STORMS

Stories and Poems

by

Gay Baines

&

Mary Ann Eichelberger

July Literary Press • Buffalo, NY • 1999
Web-Site: www.julyliterarypress.com

ACKNOWLEDGEMENTS

Grateful acknowledgment is made to the following publications where some of the contents previously appeared, as noted: The Buffalo News: "Anger," "Father," "Fire," "First Grandchild," "Heartbreak," "History (North Buffalo)," "Mars Over Bowen Road," "Moon While Tossing Out Mouse," "Mother's Day," "Night Mirror," "Rosy," "Route 240," "Scheherazade"; Cows Bigger Than Barns: "Fire"; The Croton Review: "Exit, Pursued By A Bear"; East Aurora Advertiser: "Cam & Felice," "Uncle Frank"; ELF: Eclectic Literary Forum: "First Moonset," "Walking After the Blizzard," "When You Think I'm Old"; Ezra Pound In Memoriam: an Anthology of Contemporary Poetry: "Ophelia Surfacing"; Fan: A Baseball Magazine: "Heartbreak"; Hodge Podge Poetry: "Moon While Tossing Out Mouse"; Icarus: "Earthly Heaviness"; Kiosk: "Ophelia Surfacing"; Room Of Our Own: "Anger," "Birth," "For a Son's Sixteenth Birthday," "Rosy," "When You Think I'm Old"; The Roycroft Review: "Finnegan's Bridge," "Mary's Violet Eyes"; The Sandhills Review: "After the Philharmonic"; Up Against the Wall, Mother: "Birth," "Route 240"; Z Miscellaneous: "Father".

Cover painting by Clare Poth

Copyright 1999 by Gay Baines and Mary Ann Eichelberger

Orffeo Printing Co., Inc. • 4490 Broadway • Depew, NY 14043

Table of Contents

Gay Baines

STORIES

Cam & Felice 9
Finnegan's Bridge 15
Mary's Violet Eyes 23
Uncle Frank 36

POEMS

Walking After The Blizzard 43
History (North Buffalo) 44
After The Philharmonic 46
Birth 47
Anger 48
Route 240 49
Heartbreak 50
Night Mirror 51
Scheherazade 52
Ophelia Surfacing 54
Exit, Pursued By A bear 55
Earthly Heaviness 56
Rosy 57
Mars Over Bowen Road 58
First Moonset 59
Moon While Tossing Out Mouse 60
Fire 61

Table of Contents

Mary Ann Eichelberg

Stories

Mother's Candy Jar 65
After The Storm 76
The Broken Bowl 83
The Old Couple 92
A Cloud Slipped Across The Moon 99
Sunday Morning Sex 108
Power Play 118

Poems

Father 127
Mother's Day 128
For My Son's Sixteenth Birthday 129
First Grandchild 130
When You Think I'm Old 131

Stories

by

Gay Baines

Cam & Felice

Cam stepped from his porch, intending to walk to the corner and back. When he got to Felice's house, two doors down, he went up the narrow gravel walk and sat on the steps. It was a fresh October morning, sixty degrees. He pulled out a white handkerchief to mop his brow.

Felice looked out her window. Cam sat, erect, hands on knees, gazing defiantly out at the street. She opened her door.

"Come on in, Cam," she said, "let's talk."

They sat in her front room, which had a bay window, a remote TV, an Empire couch, and a black marble mantelpiece. On the mantle was a square Victorian clock with gilt hands. Cam knew this room almost as well as he knew his own kitchen.

"How are things?" Felice asked.

"I've given up practicing law," he said, "but you know that. And I've got to sell my house."

"Really."

"Bills keep coming in. Gotta sell. Hate to do it."

"Maybe your tenants upstairs will buy it."

"Wish they would. I think my price is too high. Two hundred thousand. What do you think, Felice?"

"Sounds fair."

Felice was ninety-one. People said she looked seventy, making her laugh. She had been a schoolteacher, the legendary sort that people remember all their lives. Her quick temper lay behind her mild exterior like a deep pool. In Paterson's School 36 she had taught ten-year-olds to memorize Shakespeare and Wordsworth. She had trained sixth-graders to sing four-part harmony. She had marched her classes to museums and libraries, made them learn from the very stones they trod.

Her late husband, Fred, had married the laughing Irish girl with green eyes and auburn hair who sold stockings in Meyers' on Saturdays and told fortunes on weekends at Lake Hopatcong. He didn't know the teacher whose glance could kill. Fred was a kidder. He kidded Felice all through their fifty-five year marriage.

Felice ate it up. Their four children fled to distant cities so Felice couldn't keep an eye on them. Every few months they came home, at first to see Fred, later to sample Felice's chocolate bonbon cake. Then they rushed back home. Felice used to moan that they lived too far away, but Fred said "They're better off. Goshen's a good place to be *from*."

Cam was one year younger than Felice and, like her, born in Jersey. He grew up in Mahwah, a small town compared to Paterson. He got his law degree at NYU, and moved to Goshen, sixty miles northwest of Manhattan. Goshen was even smaller than Mahwah. He bought a brick townhouse on Attorney Row. In those days he was a spare, wiry young man with springy hair, beady eyes, and high cheekbones. The house on Attorney Row had three apartments. Cam rented the top two flats and kept the first floor for himself. His office was in the front room. There was one room in the back, and a small kitchen. He kept a bottle of milk on the windowsill in winter, a bag of oranges in the icebox. He bought ice only on weekends, in case he wanted a glass of Jack Daniels. He put his money in savings.

The County Building was fifteen steps away, County Court across the street, the Hudson Diner down a block, the Goshen Cinema around the corner, the Post Office a brisk five block walk. Across from the Post Office was the Erie Railroad station with its sign GOSHEN HOME OF THE HAMBLETONIAN.

Every third weekend Cam rode the Erie down to Mahwah to see his cousin Pat, whom he was courting. After three years, tired of eating out, of living behind his office, he married Pat and bought a big green house way out Main Street. Pat redecorated the house. She was a smart girl who made her own clothes from Vogue patterns. Once a month she and Cam took the Erie to New York to see a show, eat at Longchamps, buy shoes. They had no children. When they had lived on Main Street for five years, Felice and Fred bought the house two doors down.

Cam liked Fred. He trusted Felice, and enjoyed the pies she gave him and Pat for Sunday dinner. Sometimes they would drop in on each other on summer evenings, sit in wicker chairs on the porch, watch cars go by, talk about the war just ended, speculate on the weather. Afterwards Felice would say to Fred "Well, she's certainly queen in that house." Cam would say to Pat "She's got him where she wants him, all right. Poor Fred." But Fred was happy, and Cam adored Pat.

Cam and Fred went to village ball games together, commiserated over painting their houses. Cam bought expensive paintbrushes, painted with exactitude in smooth square strokes. When he was finished he cleaned the brushes in turpentine and hung them on long nails above the neat table in his cellar workshop. Fred picked up brushes cheap and threw them away after he finished painting. Cam mowed his grass weekly, swept up the clippings, and attacked weeds with tools and chemicals. Fred mowed his grass when he had the time, let the clippings lie among the crabgrass and dandelions flourishing on his lawn. "They're just as green as the grass," he said. "Let 'em stay." His lawn was just as lush as Cam's, but Cam bore him no ill will.

As a girl, Felice looked older than her age. Not until she was very old did people exclaim at her youthful appearance. This paradox was not lost on her. She had always been plump. Women of sixty and seventy, with birch-thin figures, envied her deceptively fertile look. Pat did not achieve Felice's vast age, and never suffered the indignity of sagging flesh. Her last illness purified her slender elegance. No one save Cam ever saw her without makeup, without her dark hair curved in its smooth pageboy.

Cam and Fred were friends, but Pat and Felice lived on different mental streets. They envied each other's kitchens. Pat envied Felice's apparent placidity. Felice envied Pat her ability to sew. They did kind things for each other. Felice's terrier Saxifrage once chased an escaped murderer away from the neighborhood. In gratitude Pat sent Felice a dozen roses. Felice sent Pat a lemon angel pie when a marron soufflé Pat had made fell flat just before an important dinner. They exchanged recipes and remedies. Yet a wall remained between them. It was not jealousy, for both women were beautiful. It was not disappointment, for both were happy. It was not intellect, for both had been teachers. It was not a trait, nor was it class, nor temperament. The wall was a process and a history: Felice had children and Pat did not.

"Just as well," Fred used to say. "They're too fussy, the both of them. Kids would drive them crazy."

"If they had kids they wouldn't be so fussy," Felice said. "They'd learn to be casual, like us."

"You? Casual?" Fred said. "Hah! Felice the Storm Trooper? The Martinet?"

"Oh, go on," Felice said, and they both laughed.

Pat died young, of myasthenia gravis. At first she couldn't talk, then she couldn't swallow. Finally she couldn't breathe.

Felice shook her head. "I saw Pat yesterday," she said to Fred, "and she can barely move, but she looked like a fashion model. Not a wrinkle, lipstick perfect, every hair in place." She took Cam and Pat roast beef, cheese cobbler, quince jam, fresh peach pie. After Pat's death in Columbia-Presbyterian Hospital, Cam came back to live alone in his house. He rented the upstairs to nice young couples with dogs and children. He planted arborvitae along the north side of his property. He learned to cook, and ate his simple broiled meals alone, off the Spode wedding china he and Pat had always used. His hair thinned. On fine days he walked the half-mile to his office. He remained spare, wiry, erect. Felice and Fred invited him over once a week for dinner.

Fred grew frail and died despite Felice's valiant efforts to keep him alive. She stayed on in her house. She had no tenants. Her life was a simple one in elaborate surroundings, like a thread of silk drawn through a square of re-embroidered lace. Like Cam, she pared away, but not to the point of true thinness. Thanks to her children and to Fred's Dutch way with money, she lived well, had a cleaning lady twice a month, and a man in once a week to mow the lawn, plow the walk, take her shopping. She developed a philosophy: at her age, she could eat, wear, say, and do what she liked, and apologized to nobody.

At the dark of the year, in mid-March, Cam became ill and was taken to the hospital. Felice did not see him for two months. He would not permit flowers, calls, cards, or any other forms of sympathy. Felice kept her distance. The finance company towed away Cam's new Accord. Eventually he came home, and lived as before, except that his meals were delivered. Felice wanted to send food to him but could not figure how to do it. After a few weeks she phoned him.

"I'm doing fine," he said briskly. She left it at that.

Now it was autumn. During his last visit to the doctor, Cam had complained of difficulty walking.

"Exercise then," the doctor said, in the brusque way reserved for very old patients. "Get out and walk." So Cam walked, or started to, and ended up at Felice's house.

"Tea?" Felice asked.

"Don't mind if I do."

As they drank tea and ate Spritz cookies, Felice brought up the subject of Cam's house again.

"You listed the property yet?"

"No. Called them yesterday. It takes time."

Felice hesitated before going on. "Cam," she said, "why don't you sell your other property?"

"My office?"

"Sure. It's business property. It'll bring you more. And you have that other lot, next to the Inn. The income can pay the taxes on your house."

"You're right," he said. "Dammit, Felice, I'm a lawyer. I should have thought of that."

"Fred taught me a few things," Felice said, simpering a little, in a way her daughters found irritating. "If you've given up your practice, you won't need an office. But you do need a place to live. Keep your house, Cam. Without it you're just a statistic." Felice, who was half-English, believed in property. Except where the law was concerned, Cam never thought about it one way or another.

"Now you can help *me* out," Felice said. "I got some darn thing from the government the other day and can't read the fine print."

"Give it to me," Cam said. He took the flimsy sheets and scanned them quickly. "Good news," he said. "It's the IRS. They made an error in July. You'll be getting a check."

"I can't believe it," Felice said. "How much?"

"Twenty-nine dollars," Cam said.

"Oh," said Felice. "Well, it's twenty-nine I didn't have when I woke up this morning."

"Invest it, Felice. That's high-flown lawyer's advice. I'd better go, read my own mail. You need any reading done, let me know. Maybe I can get my blasted legs to work if I drop in and read your mail every day or so."

"Good. And I can walk. Not fast, but I can still do it. So if you need anything--"

"Next time you're in Strong's, pick me up a cane, will you? I'll pay you back."

"So long as it's less than twenty-nine dollars."

They laughed.

"Off I go," Cam said. "You watching the baseball playoffs tomorrow?"

"Yes. Come on down and we can watch it together. I'll show you how to keep a box score."

They stood at the door. The house, built in 1876, surrounded them with its high ceilings, plaster moldings, and narrow windows. Cam and Felice looked out from its hushed scented dimness through the frosted glass of the door. Outside, flicked by wind, stood garnet-tipped maples.

"We're like the leaves at the top of the tree, you and I," Cam said. "We're still hanging on. Who knows when we'll fall?"

"Think of the lovely journey to the ground," Felice said.

Finnegans Bridge

After Patrick died Marnie was desolate. More than that, she was angry. People were kind to her, brought her casseroles and angel cakes, sent her cards and bouquets. They telephoned her, told her how much they loved her, how much they had admired Patrick. When they left her alone Marnie sat on the screen porch looking out at the woods. She drank Savory & James cream sherry from a square glass tumbler and cursed Patrick under her breath.

"You bastard," she muttered. "How could you?" She had an idea, which she knew was crazy, that Patrick's spirit hovered somewhere out there in the woods. They had bought the house because of the woods. Patrick took Marnie on long walks through the trees, making new paths in the brush and mud. He pointed out special plants or tracks of the beasts and birds that lived there. The woods belonged to Patrick. They were his kingdom, and he ruled them benignly.

Now that Patrick was dead the woods belonged to Marnie. Since he was no longer here to talk her through them, to bend down and lift up striped stones and explain where they came from, Marnie did not want to go into the woods. She let the narrow paths, spotted with newly fallen leaves, grow together again. A real estate agent came to learn if she wanted to sell any of the land. She sent him away.

When he knew he was dying, Patrick had said "We should make a plan for you, so you won't be unhappy. This society destroys single people, especially widows." The first list included "Things to Do": weave a rug for the study, catalog the book collection, go to law school, bake bread and sell it at the Country Market. The second list was "Things to Join": the local chapter of the AAUW, Citizens Against Nuclear Power, Friends of the Library. The third list was "Things to be Done to the House with the Insurance Money": install new locks, have insulation blown in, build a new garage, have the yard landscaped. There was a fourth list, but Marnie didn't want to look at it. She stared at the lists, written in Patrick's neat italic, and was too numb to understand them. The lists had reassured her when Patrick was dying, but now he was dead they seemed like instructions written on a wall by an invisible hand.

After a few weeks she ran out of Savory & James. She couldn't bear to sit on the porch without it so she put on her trekkers and walked into town. Her intention was to stop at the yarn shop and buy wool to weave a rug. On the edge of town she saw a sign, "Puppies $5," leaning against a display of tires at the Citgo station. The puppies were half husky, half golden retriever. At three months they were scrambly balls of fur. Marnie picked out one of the smaller ones. He was a rich sable color. She named him Dmitri.

Patrick had not suggested she get a dog. He had installed a burglar alarm which he said was worth two watchdogs. But the little blinking red lights on the alarm were no company for Marnie. Dmitri was company. Not as elegant as Patrick, not as soft-spoken, not at all brilliant. But he was lively and uncritical. He got along with Maddy and Fedora, the cats. Maddy (originally Maddalena) was a sprightly calico, Fedora a dark quiet Burmese. Like Dmitri they were uncritical, Marnie thought, and then wondered why she concentrated so on lack of criticism.

The day after she bought Dmitri she realized she had forgotten to buy sherry, so she got in the Volvo and drove to the liquor store. The windows and walls were decorated in orange and black crepe paper. Bottles of Sangria and Beaujolais sat slantwise in plastic pumpkins. Patrick would have looked around and made dry comments, but Marnie could thing of nothing. While she was paying for her Savory & James, a man came in who was very tan and wore a long stringy muffler wound around his neck many times, the fringed ends dangling down in back of the hood of his Indiana University sweatshirt. He smiled at Marnie with large even teeth and said "Cass! Great! Thought you'd never get here. How's everything back home?" He started to talk about the awful weather here in upstate New York, but Marnie stopped him.

"I'm not Cass," she said.

He apologized. "Sorry, you look like her, or at least I thought you did." When Marnie looked puzzled he explained: "Cassandra Yale. The actress."

"Oh," Marnie said.

"We're shooting a film here, at the race track, but Cass has been dawdling out on the coast. She's got this little kid she dotes on, see. Let me introduce myself. I'm Phil Martingale. Director of Photography."

Marnie was impressed. She had done some film studies at the university. "I'm Margaret--Marnie--Spiggott," she said. "I know your work." This was a lie. She wondered if she should say something about production values or suture, but thought better of it. Patrick knew all that stuff better than she did.

After Martingale left the salesclerk said "They're signing up extras at the Masonic Temple. Why don't you try it?"

"I don't think so," Marnie said. She went home, fed the cats and walked Dmitri. It was too cold to sit on the porch, so she sat by the windows upstairs, looking out at the woods and cursing Patrick. She thought of him sorrowing above the softness of the trees at the very idea of her being an extra in a film.

When her glass was empty she looked in the closet for yarn. There was none; but lying on its side, its pendulum taped to its back, was the mantel clock she had inherited from her rich aunt Mamie. Patrick had not thought much of clocks, calling them "gadgets."

"But you have a watch," Marnie had objected.

"Yes, but it needs no winding," he said. "Wind-up clocks are a nuisance. They take up time better spent reading." And he returned to his Descartes.

Marnie took the clock downstairs and placed it in the center of the mantelpiece. She hooked the pendulum, inserted the brass key and wound the spring, then the strike. Bang bang went the clock. She moved the hands to the correct time to match the strike, then set the hands at the current hour. It was five to six. In a few minutes the clock struck again. Bang Bang Bang Bang Bang Bang.

Dmitri let out a sharp woof. Marnie scrambled two eggs, made a salad and sat down to eat them with bread and wine, listening to the ticking of the clock, the purring of the cats. She thought: After twenty years of listening to Patrick discuss Yeats or the impact of the twentieth century on the novel as a form, or the life cycle of the Atlantic medusa, here I am listening to conversation consisting of "Tick tock," "Bang Bang," "Woof," and "Grom." Tomorrow, she decided, she would join the Friends of the Library. Before going to bed she drank some more Savory & James with two Valium. As these agents drew her into sleep she lay on her side of the double bed and said "Damn you," aloud to Patrick whom she still thought of as hovering out back in the woods.

The next day she set out for the Library to ask about the Friends. On the way there she saw a crowd of people lining up at the Masonic Temple. She parked the car and stood with them.

As they stood in line, waiting for bored girls behind long tables to take their names, Marnie asked the young woman next to her "What movie are they making?"

"It's a remake of *Dark Victory*," the young woman said.

"What?"

When it was Marnie's turn at the long table, the bored girl didn't even look up. She took Marnie's name, address, telephone and Social Security numbers, and asked if she belonged to Actor's Equity. Marnie said no and signed a paper that the girl thrust at her.

"Wait over there. You'll be called," the girl said.

Marnie waited. For a while she read *The Magic Mountain*, which had been one of Patrick's favorite books. He had recommended several times that she read it. She put it in the pocket of her down vest when the woman next to her asked a question.

"Did you see the truck?"

"No."

"It's huge. They parked it near the tennis courts. They're going to film a game later today."

"Is there a tennis game in *Dark Victory*?" Marnie asked. She was sure that the only sport in the original film was horseback riding.

"*Dark Victory*? I thought it was a remake of *Now, Voyager*."

Marnie was not called. At five she went home, fed the cats, walked Dmitri, ate supper while doing a crossword puzzle. Then she lit a fire in the Franklin stove and stared at the smoked glass, cursing Patrick. She began to think of Patrick's spirit as embodied in the burning logs. The clock banged ten times. The cats purred. Dmitri slept on the hearth rug. Marnie went to bed and, as she fell asleep, realized she hadn't joined the Friends of the Library.

The leaves were turning in the woods. "Aren't they lovely?" her neighbor asked the next morning. Marnie hated watching leaves turn. She remembered how, in grade school, she had had to collect five beautiful leaves to bring to class. All the children tried to outdo each other in producing the most gorgeous leaves. It seemed unfair to Marnie. Her parents' house had been surrounded by horse chestnut trees which dropped mahogany nuts with spiny green caps but sprouted large long leaves which turned a dull yellow in the fall. Marnie gathered her leaves from the sidewalk on the way home from school. In class the leaves were pasted in a book, or coated with wax, or sprayed with a strong varnish that smelled of bananas. It all seemed very silly to her now. She looked out at the reddening maples and shimmering birches in Patrick's woods and wondered if he would keep one tree's leaves green for her. That's a silly idea, too, she thought.

The clock banged. She left the house and drove back to the Masonic Temple, waited, read, went out to lunch, waited again. At 3:15 she was called. Phil Martingale sat on the stage of the Masonic Auditorium with other men, all dressed in expensive rumpled clothes. Martingale did not seem to remember her.

"Have you appeared as an extra in any previous Vega productions, Miz Spiggott?" asked one of the men.

"No," she said.

"She looks a little like Cass," Phil Martingale said. "Turn your head, dear."

She bridled but complied.

"Yeah, she could be her stand-in."

The next day Marnie had to be at the race track at ten o'clock. She was there, but nobody paid any attention to her.

Everyone eventually was given lunch, which was surprisingly good, served buffet style on long tables. The sun warmed Marnie's hair as she ate chicken salad and drank coffee. After lunch they called her name and asked her to stand in one of the boxes among the pigeon droppings. They gave her a floppy hat two sizes too large.

"Look up," they said, then "Okay, good. Now look out at the track. Now look toward the camera."

"What *is* this film?" she asked one of the other people who waited with her.

"I think it's a remake of *Letters to a Stranger*," came the reply. "They told me Harrison Ford has the Gary Merrill part."

Marnie was tired when Dmitri barked at the door for his walk. She took him anyway. My life is without form, and void, she thought. When she got home she got out Patrick's lists, looked at them and sighed. They were the outline of her life, but she was spilling out over the edges, like a child's watercolor.

The next day she was in a crowd scene with a hundred other people from the village. They gathered on the track in front of the judge's stand.

"All right," shouted Phil Martingale. "You're all listening to a speech, see? I want you to cheer, or boo, or whatever you like. Let's try it once."

They all yelled. Most of the other people shouted "Yaaay!" so Marnie did too. But much later, when the light was perfect, and the cameras were rolling, she found herself screaming obscenities, shaking her fist, pulling her face into a mask of hate. When the shooting was over, she wondered if, having shaken her fist on film, she had acquired a kind of thin immortality.

"Thank you very much," shouted Martingale. "Be back tomorrow, everyone."

As Marnie walked toward the parking lot, Phil Martingale approached her.

"I watched you in the crowd scene," he said. "You looked really angry."

"I probably was," she said.

"Oh, I thought it was acting. Your own home-grown

method."

He laughed. She looked at him. He seemed younger than she had remembered.

That night, as the clock banged eight times, she got out Patrick's fourth list: "Checking out a Second Husband." The list read: 1. Must be younger than you are or you die alone. 2. Must have a college education. 3. Must have a good job. 4. Must share our interests, *e.g.* reading, philosophy, film noir.

Marnie sat up late that night, looking out at the black huddle of woods. Damn you, she thought. Why didn't I argue with you when you were alive? You and your bloody programs for living. These thoughts alarmed her at first, but then Dmitri nuzzled her hand.

The next day Phil Martingale asked to see where she lived. She drove him out to her house. It was a warm day with a dramatic sky flying past a falling November sun. Phil turned his nose immediately toward the woods, exclaimed at their beauty, and asked who lived over that way.

"Nobody," she said. "They're my husband's woods." The moment she said it she felt stupid. "I mean, of course, they're mine now," she added, feeling her face turn pink.

"Let's go walk in them," he said, and took her hand, leading her back into the thicket at the edge of the stand of birches, firs, and maples of which Patrick had been so proud. He'll see us here, she thought, and then remembered that this was not possible.

Tramping through the brush and fallen leaves, she felt at first an ache of nostalgia for the walks with Patrick. Then she remembered how those walks had diminished her.

"See that striped tree over there?" she asked. He stopped and stared. "It's a moosewood. Look at the pointed leaves. It's related to the maple."

"I didn't know that," he said, as Marnie had said in the past.

"One thing I've been wanting to ask you," she said. "What movie are you making? Everybody says it's a remake of this, a remake of that. It makes no sense to me."

His face looked shocked. "It's not a remake at all," he said. "It's a totally new concept. The working title is *Finnegan's*

Bridge."

"Sounds like a card game you play after coming home from Finnegan's Wake," she said. It was a joke Patrick might have made, that she might have laughed at. Phil Martingale laughed.

"I don't believe you're the D.P. on this film at all," she said.

"You're right. I'm third--no, fourth--assistant to the director. One slip and I'll be out of a job," he said. He was jittery in the woods. "I didn't know woods were so messy," he said. "Out on the coast the woods are dry, the floors smooth, like concrete. You could set up housekeeping in them." He looked down at the mud on his loafers. "This is a wet place," he said.

Marnie took him back to the house, gave him a brush to clean his loafers with and set out tea and a plate of madeleines. He seemed to want more, but she felt careless about his wants in a way she had never felt about Patrick's wants. She liked the idea; it filled her mind with fresh air.

Dmitri, who had put his snout on Phil's knee, suddenly barked. Marnie stood up. "I must walk Dmitri," she said.

"I'd go with you," Phil said, "but I have a date for dinner. Can I walk back to town?"

"It's a mile. You could walk it, but I'll take you," she said.

"No, I'll walk." As he put on his coat he said, again, "You were really angry today. In the crowd scene."

"Yes," she said. "I'm angry at Patrick." She waited a beat, then added "Because he died."

"Is that it really?" he said.

He'll do for a start, she thought as he set out in his freshly-cleaned loafers toward the village. When she unlocked the door after walking Dmitri, she heard the clock bang six times. She poured a glass of ruby port and went upstairs. The woods were burnished by the afterlight of the sunset.

"Well, Patrick," she said. "I'm still here."

Mary's Violet Eyes

When Devlin and I went out together, we followed a strange schedule. He picked me up at six-thirty p.m. and drove me to breakfast at Tamara and Joe's Diner in Ames Plaza. Depending on the time of year we would watch the natural light fade or the junky lights of the plaza grow brighter. Then we'd go for a walk until it was time for him to report to the Observatory at eleven. He and another astronomer took turns sitting in the telescope, watching the sky and freezing. During the winter he went to work in an old hooded parka and ragg gloves with the fingers cut off. He had singed the edges of the cut-off fingers with a wooden kitchen match. When I told him I hadn't realized that being an astronomer would mean sitting about in the cold all night, he said gloomily, "Neither did I."

Devlin liked his job, though. He liked working alone, sleeping during the day and being up at night. His apartment was in a barn on Kirkby's farm out on the Scotchtown Road. The ground floor of the barn housed Kirkby's farm machines. The second floor had two apartments. Mr. Dunwoodie, the high school math teacher, lived in the other apartment with his wife and two children.

The floors of the barn apartments were cold. Devlin and the Dunwoodies kept trying to think of ways to make them warmer. I pointed out to Devlin that between living in Kirkby's barn and working at the Observatory, he spent most of the winter months freezing. He agreed with me, but didn't do much about it except drink lots of coffee with sugar and condensed milk, which made him excitable.

One Saturday in mid-December I drove out to Devlin's place with the makings of dinner in a basket: lamb chops, macaroni salad, French bread, a jar of homemade tomato soup, carrot sticks, a raspberry pie, and two bottles of champagne. Devlin had promised to provide butter, baked potatoes, and ice cream for the pie. When I arrived he was playing chess with Mr. Dunwoodie.

"Have you put in the potatoes?" I asked.

"No," he said. Devlin always talked like a robot when he

played chess. I had expected him to forget the potatoes, so I turned the oven on high, put the potatoes in, and began setting the table.

Devlin lost a game to Mr. Dunwoodie, played a second one, lost again, and then put the chessboard away. He came out into the kitchen, looking sneaky.

"Dunwoodie's had a fight with his wife," he said. "I promised to put him up. He hasn't any place to go."

"Oh, fine," I said.

"There's more," Devlin said. "His wife is holding his lecture notes hostage."

"That's ridiculous," I said.

"Well, that's what he says," Devlin said. "Can we have three for dinner?"

"I already figured on that," I said. "Open the champagne. Maybe it'll cheer him up."

Devlin got out the shrimp cocktail glasses that he used for champagne. Then he popped open the bottle, and brought the wine into the living room. Mr. Dunwoodie was watching the news disconsolately. He accepted his glass without paying much attention but his face brightened when he tasted the bubbly wine.

"Nice," he said.

I whisked the lambchops into the broiler, laid the table, sliced the bread, set out the salads, and in half an hour we were eating dinner and drinking the rest of the champagne, which was domestic and fruity, but not bad for a Saturday night supper in the upstairs of a barn on Scotchtown Road.

Mr. Dunwoodie shook his head as he ate. "NASA had to scratch another space shuttle," he said. "It's a crying shame." He seemed more depressed over this news than he did over the mess in the Middle East, the increasing numbers of homeless, or even over the fight with his wife and the captivity of his math notes.

"Isn't this telescope in space kind of a frill?" I asked.

The men stared at me, munching.

"Certainly not," Mr. Dunwoodie said.

"We need to explore, to probe the outer reaches of the stars," Devlin said.

They were both astronomers of a kind. Mr. Dunwoodie kept a small tripod telescope on the porch of his apartment. He could use it only in the warmer months. Right now the telescope was packed away. Or being held hostage.

"I don't know a thing about stars," I said. "All I can remember from grade school is 'Mary's violet eyes.'"

They stared at me again. "Mary's violet eyes?" Devlin said.

"'Mary's Violet Eyes Make John Stay Up Nights Pluto,'" I said. "Everybody learns that."

"Oh, yeah," Mr. D. said, but Devlin still looked confused.

"What does that mean?" he asked.

"It's a code. Follow the initials. They're the same as the planets, starting from the sun. Mercury Venus Earth Mars and so forth. Except it's so old they thought it up before Pluto was discovered, so 'Pluto' is tacked on at the end."

Devlin was totally at sea. Mr. Dunwoodie recited softly to himself: "Mary's violent eyes make John stay up nights. Pluto."

"'Violet,'" I said, "not 'violent.'"

"It makes sense," he said, paying no attention to me.

"Mary's violet eyes," I said. "Nobody would have violent eyes. Violet."

"Nobody has violet eyes either," Devlin objected.

"Elizabeth Taylor does," I said.

"Mercury Venus Earth Mars Jupiter Saturn Neptune Pluto," Mr. Dunwoodie chanted.

"I didn't know that," Devlin said.

Mr. Dunwoodie and I looked at him. "Know what?" I asked.

"That Liz Taylor has violent eyes," he said.

"VIOLET, not violent," I said. "Take my word for it. Or look it up if you don't believe me. She has purple eyes, but they always call them 'violet' for some reason."

"Are you sure it isn't 'violent'?" Mr. Dunwoodie said. "I think that's the way I learned it."

"Had they discovered Pluto when you were a kid?" I said cruelly.

"Of course they had," he said in a hurt voice.

"Well, there you are. Back in the days before Pluto was discovered, they wouldn't have used 'violent.'"

"I don't know. Think of the suffragettes," Devlin said.

"It's suffragists, Devlin," I said, "and they might have been violent, but their eyes weren't."

We finished the champagne and washed the dishes. Then we sat on Devlin's lumpy furniture and wondered what to do.

Finally I said "Let's go rescue Dunwoodie's lecture notes." The men protested feebly. It was no use, they said. Lurlene (Mrs. D.) was too clever, too angry, too this, too that. I put on my Maggie Thatcher face and strode out to the corridor, where I knocked on the Dunwoodies' door. Lurlene answered. She was a pretty, Wagnerian blonde in a purple dressing gown, holding a snifter of brandy. This unnerved me, but only slightly.

"Dunwoodie wants his lecture notes," I said.

"Okay," Lurlene said affably and disappeared for a few seconds. She returned with a battered briefcase. "Here they are."

I took the notes back to Devlin's flat. "You idiots," I said. "Here are your lecture notes, Dunwoodie. Why didn't you just ask for the darn things?"

He seized the briefcase with relief and opened it. "I've got to review some of this stuff," he said. "Can I use your study, Devlin?"

Devlin and I went for a walk, over the plank path leading out to Kirkby's woods. Our feet made sharp new holes in the snow. Walking at night in winter was one of Devlin's tricks for keeping warm in his apartment. He figured that after being outside in below-freezing temperatures, anything indoors would seem warm, even Kirkby's cold barn.

I looked up at the sky. Devlin tended to ignore stars when he wasn't working, but I found them more and more interesting, perhaps because of Devlin, perhaps not.

"There's Orion," I said, looking almost straight overhead.

"Everybody knows Orion," he said in a dissatisfied voice.

"Of course. Ordinary, non-astronomer persons like me have to have an easy identifier, like the three stars in his belt," I said. "The dogs are another matter. How the ancient Greeks could turn two stars into one dog is more than I can see."

"That's all poppycock," he said.

"What system do you use?" I asked.

"We use the constellations as references," he said, "but we have a system of enumeration for all the various phenomena."

"Ah, you scientists, always de-romanticizing," I said.

"It isn't romance," he said. "The ancient Greeks and Egyptians--they took it seriously. We call it mythology. It was their religion, their faith, they believed it all."

He had me there, I thought. "I just meant using numbers," I said. "It sounds so dull."

"Not much different from your 'Mary's violent eyes,'" he said.

"It's 'violet,' dammit, Devlin."

"I think 'violent' sounds better," he said stubbornly.

"But it doesn't make sense," I said. "Eyes can't be violent."

"Stars can," he said. The after-dinner coffee had wound him up again.

"Stars? Violent? I thought they just sat there," I said.

"They don't look violent," he said, "but they are. From here they just twinkle. Through the scope they're full of flame and tears."

"Flame I can see," I said, "but 'tears'? You've had too much champagne, Devlin. Besides, the initials in the chant are for planets, not stars."

"I can't explain it," he said. "Flame and tears. That's what I see up there. It's why I keep going back every night, in the dark, cold and alone."

He said no more, seemed almost embarrassed at having said this much. We went back to the barn. Maybe Devlin's theory about staying warm was true. It seemed warmer in the apartment than it had before we went out. In part the warmth must have flowed from Devlin's study. Mr. Dunwoodie came flying out, his eyes burning.

"Our discussion of 'Mary's violent eyes' gave me an idea," he said. I rolled my own eyes and went into the kitchen to make more coffee. The men followed me. Mr. D. was excited.

"It's just doggerel, Dunwoodie," Devlin said, but Mr. Dunwoodie wasn't listening.

"It all makes sense," he said. "Mary's violent eyes--that

doesn't mean some girl John is soft on. It's the burning eyes of a goddess or a saint--the Virgin Mary, say--"

"Who's 'John,' then," I said sarcastically. "John the Baptist? And why does he 'stay up nights'?"

"I haven't figured it out yet," he said. "Maybe it should be some other verb."

"What you're saying," I said, "is that we need a new code to remember the names of the planets."

"Yes," he said.

"Well, going all theological isn't going to be much help. Remember the planets are named for Greco-Roman gods."

"Here's what I've figured out," Dunwoodie said. "Minerva's Virtuous Ego Marches Jonathan Sideways Under North Philadelphia."

"You're out of your mind," I said. "Who could remember that?"

"People in Philadelphia," Devlin said. There was a knock at the door. I opened it. Dunwoodie's wife stood in the hallway, dressed in distressed-leather slacks and a big loose lavender sweater. She held a foil-covered pan.

"Hi," she said. "I made a coffee cake. It's a peace offering to Dunwoodie, but I'd like all of us to share it."

"Wonderful," I said. Did everybody call her husband "Dunwoodie"?

The four of us sat at Devlin's round kitchen table. We polished off a pot a coffee and most of Devlin's sherry as we ate the coffee cake. We talked about the weather, about birds flying north and south, the vocabulary of Dunwoodie's kids, about Christmas, which was coming, about the greenhouse effect. But I wanted to ask Lurlene something.

"It's none of my business," I said, "but why did you hold Dunwoodie's notes hostage?"

"I do that a lot," she said easily. "It gets Dunwoodie out of the house. So I can have some peace."

Dunwoodie blushed.

"Why don't you just say 'Clear out, Dunwoodie'?" I asked.

"That would be mean," she said. Apparently she meant it, too.

In some way she had Dunwoodie wrapped around her little finger. My mother would have called her a sharp petunia. But I felt sorry for her, trapped in this second floor of a barn with Dunwoodie, his telescope, and his bulging briefcase of notes.

"We were talking earlier about the doggerel we used to learn the order of the planets," I said. "Mary's violet eyes. You ever hear of it?"

"Yes," she said, "but too late."

"Too late?"

"Yes. I went to Foxboro until my junior year of high school. Then my parents split up. Mama couldn't afford to keep me in Foxboro so I spent the last two years at Washingtonville High. That's where I heard of 'Mary's violet eyes,' but I had already learned the planets."

I knew Foxboro. It was a finishing school in a nineteenth-century mansion near the cliffs of the Hudson. Washingtonville High must have been a rude awakening for Lurlene.

"How did you learn the planets?" I asked.

"I broke it up into pieces," she said. "First, I learned that Earth is the third planet."

"Okay," Devlin said. He and Mr. Dunwoodie were hanging on every word. We're all fools, I thought.

"I remembered the first two by thinking of them as the initials of the Virgin Mary, reversed."

Here we go again, I thought. "Why reversed?" I asked.

"Well, this is a man's world," she said, "so I figured it was a man's universe as well. Venus is the only feminine planet. No man would place her next to the sun."

"Of course not," I said drily.

"The next two after Earth I remembered by matching them with the first two. Another M, the first from Earth as Mercury is first from the sun. Then J, which could stand for Jesus, which would match V for Virgin."

"Or V for Venus," I put in.

"Venus was Virgin Mary to the Greeks," she said. "But in any case it helped me remember. The next three planets spell SUN, which was easy. Pluto I just remembered from the cartoons."

"You mean the dog Pluto?" Mr. Dunwoodie said.

"Yes."

He stared at her as if seeing her for the first time.

"That's kind of confusing," Devlin said. "In fact, it's a real mess. 'Mary's violent eyes' is a lot easier."

"VIOLET, dammit," I said. "What difference does it make? Just so you remember." I felt a bit miffed, not having had the advantage of a prep-school education, even a curtailed one, as Lurlene's had turned out to be. When we were out in the kitchen she had told me she'd gone to a state college and become a teacher of English, met Dunwoodie, and married him. What if she had "finished" at Foxboro, gone to Vassar or Radcliffe, married a rich lawyer, lived in a posh suburb with servants, three cars, purebred dogs, a pool, a summer place in New England, a winter condo in Florida, and a mink coat? When I had asked her that she had said she envied none of it except (considering where she lived) the mink coat.

Devlin suggested we go out on Dunwoodie's porch where (he claimed) he could point out all the stars, the visible planets, and anything else we might want to see. It sounded cold and tedious to me at first, but then I remembered his little tricks for staying warm, and went along. We bundled into boots and parkas and tracked out into the hard-packed snow on Dunwoodies' porch. Devlin had a little hand telescope, the Dunwoodies shared a pair of opera glasses, and I carried Devlin's binoculars, the ones we had used the previous summer to spy on loons in A.Y. Jackson Lake.

The stars blazed. We found Polaris easily enough, and the Dippers. Dunwoodie pointed out Cassiopeia, and joked that maybe that was the "M" that got Lurlene started on her elaborate acronym for the planets.

"It's a 'W' half the time, Dunwoodie," Lurlene said. "And now it's on its side, just a squiggle."

"Oh. Yeah."

Devlin ignored them. "There's Orion," he said, "and there are the Twins right above him. See?"

"I can't see where you're pointing," I said.

"If only my arms were longer," he said, a bit desperately.

"Show us a planet, Devlin," Lurlene said.

"Okay," he said. "See the Bull--Taurus--up to the right, above Orion's left fist?"

"I think so," I said.

"It's like a little arrowhead," Dunwoodie said. "The bright star is Aldebaran."

"Okay," Devlin said. "See that spot just to the left? Sort of yellowish? That's Mars."

"I thought Mars was red," I objected.

"Look through the glasses," he said.

I did, but the planet, which was easy to find as a dead light among the twinkling stars, still looked yellow.

"I'll say this for it," I said. "It looks warm."

Devlin also found Jupiter for us, but I couldn't see it. It was in Cancer, he claimed, but I could not make a shape out of the confusing cluster of stars. This failure disappointed me since Cancer is my sign, but I decided not to bring up any pseudo-science, especially with two science wizards on the porch.

Devlin was in his element. He showed us two orbiting bodies which could barely be discerned. They limped through the glittering sky, moving in no relation to the imperceptible movement of the galaxy. Their light was flat and tinny next to the stars. With some satisfaction Devlin identified them as orbiting spacecraft. I demanded to know exactly which craft they were, and when they were launched, but of course he didn't know that. Then he and Dunwoodie argued amiably about how much space junk was out there, and how much of it was really earth junk, and how much was "cosmic debris."

While they debated, I looked up again, thinking about the Aurora Borealis. It was the wrong time of year, of course. Everyone must see the Aurora at least once, or so I have been led to believe. I had never seen it. My Maine cousins had seen the Northern Lights many times, but they dismissed them as a mere greenish glow in the night sky. I wanted to see the varicolored curtains waving back and forth in space. The yellow dot that was Mars, the invisible Jupiter, Devlin's space junk--none of these were enough. I wanted to see more, and I was rewarded. There was a strange glow to the west, like fireworks but eerie. The shards of star spread apart and fell, or appeared to fall, for miles. Miles? It was more like light-years, I knew. I pointed, nudging Devlin's arm. As he turned his head to watch, another starburst scattered, and then another, and another. We were all gazing, our necks cranked to the side. Some of the meteors appeared to blink again and again, slowly, like fireflies. Others flashed and sparkled, then vanished as swiftly as they had appeared.

"Are those the Geminids?" I asked Devlin. He shook his head, not in negation, but amazement.

"I didn't know you'd heard of the Geminids," he said.

That stuck in my craw. "I'm going in," I said, and went in, but stopped in the Dunwoodies' dark living room, confused. Devlin had followed me.

"Marry me, Annie," he said.

"It's all right," I said.

"No, I mean it," he said.

"Are you sure?" I asked. "I'm not too stupid? Too undereducated? Too flashy? Too pushy?"

He winced with good reason. There were a million problems barring us from even living together. There was Devlin's mother, a Scarsdale matron on the prowl for the perfect wife for her perfect son. There was the fact that I had never finished college. There was Jackson, my former husband, out of my life for five years. There were Lucy and Jenny, my two babies. Jenny was still more or less a toddler, and Lucy an eight-year-old with amazing aplomb, who mothered her little sister as well or better than I could, which she had to do fairly frequently because my employer (Sigismond Control Data Limited) kept me late every evening. And of course there was the time I took for my odd evenings with Devlin. Jackson, last seen playing piccolo and flute for the Mid-Hudson Philharmonic, was a drunk. Perhaps he was repeatedly abusive, but I didn't stay to find out. He hit me once.

The curtailment of my excursion into higher education was directly attributable to this lead-headed, silver-voiced member of the Musicians' Union. His mother, Petula Beaurivage, was, surprisingly, my savior. She was the one who took me in when I had to flee, without luggage but with both girls. Jenny was eight months old at the time. Pet took my side against her own son, provided for me until I was able to move into my own place. At this very moment, as I peered at Devlin in the dark, Pet was babysitting so I could have a night out with my "nice astronomer chap," as she called him (she was Australian).

Devlin's mother was a religious bigot for whom every woman, even if she were the "right" faith was not religious enough for her son, a curious view since Devlin believed in no established god, never went to church, worshipped only at his telescope every night. For his mother, every woman who had so much as shared a cup of coffee with a man was "fast," to use her term. Needless to say, I did not suit her. It was because of me that Devlin had fled the comfort of his mother's Edwardian house to freeze upstate in Kirkby's barn. We were a bizarre couple. With my partial education gleaned from library books, with my addiction to chewing gum, with my over-made-up eyes and black stockings, I was not meant to be Devlin's wife. It seemed very clear to me now, in the dark. We had been in the dark and cold for so long, one way and another, that it seemed a perfect state for the two of us. The stars, whatever their names, were our daylight. We never saw each other except after sundown. During the hours we spent together we forgot about the rest of it. We had to. But if we were to live together, or even--heaven forfend--get married, we couldn't forget.

"It's the Geminids," Devlin said through my thoughts. "We'd have missed them if it hadn't been for you."

"Don't exaggerate."

"It's not just the Geminids," he went on. "I don't need you as a star guide. You--you shed different light on my life."

"I'll bet."

"I mean it, dammit, Annie." This was serious. Devlin never swore. His mother had seen to that, almost. "You know things about life I don't," he said.

"Some."

"I've spent my whole life studying, teaching, going to conferences. You haven't. You've been married, you can cook."

"Big deal."

"You're funny, you're honest, you've traveled even, you've been to Oregon."

"Oh, wow." But I was beginning to give in. "How do you know I won't pull a fast one on you, Devlin? Like Lurlene, holding Dunwoodie's notes hostage. How do you know I won't hold your fingerless gloves hostage?"

"Lurlene was just playing a game. We all play games with each other, to free each other up. I've nobody to play games on me. Marry me, Annie."

"Okay," I said. It was the only way to get out of the Dunwoodie's living room. One of their children, the younger one, began crying softly. I followed the sound. Devlin went with me. I found the nursery with its dim pink night light, went to the tall, old-fashioned crib and lifted the baby out. He was a nine-month-old, tall for his age, a brawny little kid with a dusting of soft hair and liquid eyes that peered at me curiously in the murk. "Is that it, pumpkin?" I said. "Was it strange voices you heard?"

"Maybe he's hungry," Devlin said in the hesitant tone he uses for world affairs.

"No, he's just puzzled," I said. "Probably heard us crashing about." We walked back and forth together, until the baby dropped off to sleep. Then I laid him in his crib, looking down at the closely-shut face with its blip of a nose, all the features dwarfed by his great cheeks. I thought how distant he was from us, how simple. My bracelets tinkled as I lifted my arm back over the rails of the crib. Devlin, his glasses slipping down his nose, looked closely at his watch. "We better go," he whispered, and we made our way back toward the balcony. The Dunwoodies, shivering, shut the door, slid its heavy brass bolt, pulled the curtains, closed off the glittering night sky.

"Gotta go," Devlin said. "We're getting married."

"Congratulations," Lurlene said, while Dunwoodie said, in a puzzled voice, "Now?"

"Later," Devlin said. "We just decided."

"That's great," Dunwoodie said. He shook hands vigorously with both of us.

"This calls for a drink," Lurlene said, and got out the brandy bottle. The evening had turned from an ordinary Saturday night supper into a kind of minor celebration. Lurlene handed the glasses around. They were Waterford crystal. I wondered what history lay behind their presence here in Kirkby's barn among the Dunwoodies' cheap furniture. We drank. My mind raced ahead, through Sunday papers, through the pot roast with Devlin at my apartment, through Devlin's helping Lucy with her homework, through his departure out Scotchtown Road for his last decent night's sleep before going to the Observatory Monday night. Could I move in with him and freeze in Kirkby's barn? Would his mother consent to the match? Would Jackson come storming into my life, waving his flute and demanding his daughters back?

While I was thinking these dour thoughts, Dunwoodie began toasting us. "Long life and the greatest of happiness to both of you," he said. "May the future be as kind to you as it has been to me and to Lurlene here. May your--"

"Oh for heaven's sake, Dunwoodie," Lurlene said. "This isn't the wedding reception. Save your speech. Just wish them good luck."

"Well, good luck then," he said sheepishly. "Bottoms up."

We drank. Having spent so much time out on the balcony, we all felt warm. The brandy was bottled flame. It made me think of Devlin's flame and tears, and I was very glad I had said yes to him. How different were we, I wondered, from our ancestors, gathering in a cave or around a village fire to celebrate the merging of two clans? How different were our speculations about the stars?

We held our glasses out to Lurlene. As she filled them I felt the presence of the stars in the room, clustering on the ceiling, looking down at us, savages in Kirkby's barn, drinking in warmth against the dark and the night.

Uncle Frank

Uncle Frank was a skeptic all his life. He went to church with his sisters and brothers, sang in the choir, took collection. But in high school he started going off to fish on Sunday mornings, hanging out with his friends or with girls on Thursday nights instead of going to choir practice. He married one of those girls, Marcy Schwenk, a saint of a woman, in church, the old Peace Lutheran Church on Liberia Road--that church is a library, now, imagine--a library on Liberia Road! Anyway, at Christmas and Easter he'd go to services as usual, with Aunt Marcy and my cousins, but when they got to the meat of the story, you know, the angels appearing to the shepherds, or the stone rolled away from the tomb, he'd lean over to Carl, his oldest, and say out of the side of his mouth "A likely story." Aunt Marcy would glare and nudge him in the ribs, but he just grinned at her.

By that time Uncle Frank was a successful businessman, owned Elbow Manufacturing on Seneca Street, but he still lived in the southtowns, bought an old farmhouse in West Falls, with lots of room for Aunt Marcy and the four kids.

One day while he was inspecting a building just purchased by his firm, next door on Seneca Street, a piece of stone fell from the roof. Missed him by that much. After that he got to sitting up late, thinking. Aunt Marcy noticed the change in him.

"What's wrong, Frank?" she asked.

"I've gotta change, Marcia," he said.

Thank heaven, Aunt Marcy thought, he's found God at last.

But no. Uncle Frank was making plans. "I'm forty years old," he said. "I don't want to die stupid. I'm going back to college."

He enrolled at the Evening School, signed up for courses in literature, history, philosophy, art, psychology and mathematics. His intention was to major in math or one of the sciences, but his interest was captured by philosophy. He liked to read passages at the dinner table, much to Aunt Marcy's annoyance.

"You'll put ideas in the kids' heads," she said.

Uncle Frank stared at her in surprise. "So? What harm can

Socrates do them? Or Descartes? or Meister Eckhardt?"

"You know what I mean."

"Don't be dumb." Uncle Frank wrote long, detailed theme papers on Savonarola, Kierkegaard, Nietzsche and Sartre, and received high grades. He admitted to me once that he never could get the hang of Heidegger. But that fact did not damage his academic career. After ten years of juggling classes, papers, and exams with his work at Elbow Manufacturing, he was awarded a B.A. in philosophy two weeks after his fiftieth birthday. Aunt Marcy didn't want to go to his graduation, but my cousins convinced her that she should go. They ended up on the six o'clock news, for Uncle Frank, it turned out, had done so well that he graduated Magna Cum Laude.

He hung his diploma on the wall of his office at Elbow Manufacturing, pointed it out with pride to anyone who came there. Apart from this display, his life did not change. Aunt Marcy sniffed. "All that money, all that work, and you got nothing for it."

"I got a fine education," he said. "All I ever wanted."

Eventually Uncle Frank retired from Elbow Manufacturing. He had been a popular figure in the office, the factory, and in his field. A huge retirement dinner was held at Vinney's Roman Renaissance Restaurant and Patio. He was given a gold watch; Aunt Marcy wore a new blue satin gown and an orchid corsage. There was dancing and merry-making afterward.

Uncle Frank had a happy retirement. He worked in his garden, took his boat out on Lake Erie. When he was sure he could afford it, he returned to college and began taking graduate seminars in philosophy. Aunt Marcy was disgusted for a time; but then she fell ill and died. Uncle Frank mourned, but he was not lonely; my cousin Carl, his wife Jenny, and their daughter Lorrie moved in with him in the old house in West Falls. He read philosophy long into the night, and discussed existentialism with the family at dinner. Jenny, who was a concert pianist, did not object to these discussions as Aunt Marcy had. She made Lorrie listen and contribute her own observations on being and nothingness. Carl wasn't sure it was a good idea. He tried to persuade Jenny that perhaps school or sports would be better topics for a young girl; but his comments sagged under the force of her arguments-- probably aided by the fact that during these discussions he was usually dressed in striped pajamas.

One evening the dinnertime chat drifted to the subject of the afterlife.

"Pastor Larsen says we go on living after we die," Lorrie said. "Do you believe that, Gramps?"

"I do not," Uncle Frank said, "though what other people believe is not my concern. If you and Pastor Larsen want to imagine heaven, you're free to do so. I suspect it's just not there."

"But what if there is an afterlife?" Jenny asked. "What would you make of it?"

"I'll tell you this," Uncle Frank said. "If I find there is life after death, I'll sure as heck let you all know about it."

Five years later Uncle Frank died, suddenly and quietly in the night, after a beautiful fall Sunday. My cousins, once over the initial grief, wondered if a church service was appropriate considering Uncle Frank's views, but, lacking an idea of another way to do it, had the funeral at Creekside Lutheran Church anyway. Pastor Larsen slyly selected biblical readings and prayers that hinted at Uncle Frank's apostasy. After the graveside service, we all went back to the church hall for a funeral lunch.

That night Carl, Jenny and Lorrie went back to the house Uncle Frank had lived in for so many years. While Jenny and Lorrie hung their coats, Carl reshelved the philosophy books Uncle Frank had been reading. Later he told me "Suppose I've got to read all that stuff now," in a gloomy voice.

So Jenny asked him "You want anything to eat before we go to bed?"

Carl said "It's kind of late," but she reminded him that the next day was Sunday, so he said "Okay, English muffins and coffee."

I'm not sure exactly how it happened, but just when Carl thought Jenny was in the kitchen, he heard a tremendous crash of pots and pans in the pantry. Naturally, he went out to investigate. He called out "Are you okay?"

Jenny said "Yes," right behind him. Gave him a real turn. He said he thought she'd fallen or dropped something in the pantry. But she hadn't even gone in the kitchen yet.

When they looked in the pantry, they found all of the pots, pans, dishes, and silverware were still in order.

Carl said "That's odd, I'm sure it came from out here."

Then Lorrie said "It's Gramps!" They were really spooked now, and she made them both jump. She went on: "Remember? Gramps said if he found out there was an afterlife he'd let us know. That was him, letting us know!"

Jenny couldn't believe it. She said "Don't be silly."

Lorrie insisted. "I'm sure it was Gramps, wasn't it?"

All Jenny could say was "I don't know."

Carl had to laugh. He said "What do you mean, you don't know?"

Jenny said "I don't believe in ghosts."

And Carl said "Neither do I." But then, just to be on the safe side, he added, "But I kind of like the idea."

POEMS

BY

GAY BAINES

Walking After The Blizzard
(February 1977; for Pearl)

Stars blaze. No one else walks the street,
sounds are smothered. They say crime goes down
after such storms. But look at the sky:
Cassiopeia, an uppity lady locked up
by her abusive husband to sit forever,
ferriswheeling round Polaris. The Archer
draws his poaching arrow, frozen in the flash
before some creature dies. Orion lifts his fist,
angry (as aren't we all) at life's vicissitudes.
The dogs run loose. The Gemini--are they
holding hands? Two crimes in one (if you know
what I mean). Who violated Leda's rights
to hatch them? And what of Daphne? Of Agamemnon?
If gods commit rape and murder, what hope have we?

In a city of five hundred thousand you are alone;
yet every eye that gazes on this hulk
of civilization, brought down by wind,
by piled-up snow on the lake, by rigidity
of office schedules, by worn-out buses,
gazes with you, as the ancient eyes
of those who painted the skies for us
gazed then. They knew in those clear days
our frailty, our beauty and our ugliness.
We can add little to that,
we can't even keep our world going.
Alone, in snow and stars
you don't despair. Hot tea
will warm you later, by and by
the snow will melt, and all the time
the pictures white-stitched across
the sky remain, reminders
of our mistakes, our hope and glory.

History (North Buffalo)

On a street where I lived for a time there walked
a man without destination,
dressed in a camel-hair coat, lizard shoes,
a pearl-grey fedora. Smoking a long cigar, he strode
up avenues and down streets, talking to whomever
was passing by or to no one. Sometimes to me.

One bright April day he stopped me
on my way to the bus to tell how,
a few years ago, he and another boy
he didn't name had climbed the picket fence
of that house there--he pointed:
a square brown-and-white shingle with a mansard roof--
and stole cherries from a tree in the back yard.
I squinted down at the house and saw in the yard
no trees, only a shed beyond the wood fence with Spanish posts
which demarcated the property from Mr. Oil Change.

Another time as I walked past a store marked
"Eugene's Joke Shop, established 1945,"
he turned from regarding it and said,
perhaps to me, "This used to be
Klein's Delicatessen." I hurried on. I had no use for history,
and yet I could imagine: Klein's Deli, a window with
foreign markings, an odor of pickles and corned beef;
the backyard cherries, dark, with hard stones, gone,
remembered by me though I had never seen them.

I saw him one more time: on a day in high summer, under the
    awning
at Mulligan's for a vermouth cassis on my way home.
Sitting in afternoon light, watching the sun drop
over the northwest end of Hertel, I saw him again,
wearing a Panama hat and ice cream pants, silk sleeves rolled up
    neatly,
seizing a young man by the arm, pointing across
to a grimy brick garage, telling some garbled story.
I had a vision of a palisade of thick elms raising full-leafed
    branches.
The young man blinked, frowned and tried to flee. Like
    butterflies
we are, I thought, sending my thoughts out to him. You and I,
we fly away. The young man flew away,
but the man in the crisp summer hat stood, smiling his mad
    smile,
his face sun-warmed, his legs apart,
feet planted firmly on the solid earth, fixed.

October 26: After The Philharmonic

The music could have been a warning.
Prokofiev's Fifth, its opening grandeur,
its agonies, its playful tapping end.

Sort of like the drive home. I'd arrived
in cool sun, ice clouds moving in,
came out to tin rain, nailheads
all over the windows. Cold, too,
and dark, daylight no longer saved.

So I drove home listening
to the shirring of tires on black streets,
the drum of a million
fingers on the roof,
the fuss of fans, wipers, hot stripes
in the rear window.

The car in the garage, I realized
brush clippings had to be put out
for Monday morning. Still in my
concert clothes, I carried them,
damp knotted branches still dripping
crisp green leaves.

I kept thinking of the concert,
me gazing down through opera glasses,
watching the winds, the closed face
of the pianist; feeling the warmth
of the hall, soft light on blond walls,

the timpanist. The way
he calmly selected his padded sticks,
how he touched the drums lightly,
their grave sound carrying through the
thin curtain of stringed instruments,
how he spread his hands on the smooth
skin of the drums, a quick soft touch,
quieting them.

BIRTH

They'll soak snowy cloths
in boiling water, as in the old days,
for me. I know the sting
of steaming compresses is nothing
to the other pain. I'll welcome both:
tissues dissolving from packed heat;
the harder throes cracking my shell,
spilling blood, giving life.

When I am done (or undone) they will drown
the rags again, squeeze them,
snap them in wind by the creek
then hang them up to dry in the winter sun.

Anger

Anger must be starved,
locked in a cage,
barricaded in a garret,
banished to a grey
damp-smelling shed
deep in the bush.

Give it nothing.
Let it fend for itself,
eat jewelweed and mullein,
brew fir-needles
to keep itself alive.

Give it nothing.
Anger emaciated
is wiry and tough.
It can live on scraps
or eat its own heart.

It will grow strong,
break out of its bars,
crack your castiron locks,
trek savannahs,
ford millstreams
and come back
to serve you forever.

ROUTE 240

This is the culvert where that lady died,
Flung out and bruised in snow,
Senseless and dead in snow
Pink from the dust laid down by August rains. Little did she
    know,
Tying her wool plaid scarf in wind by the farmhouse door,
How could she know that was
The last she'd ever see of her dark grey firs;
Thinking that later on that day she'd spade
That antique urn by the stoop full of draggled leaves
(Bright petunias they were in June). The same
Winter that killed her hardy annuals
Killed this daughter of soil. A patch of thin
Pale ice underneath the bridge forever doomed
That urn to rust and ash-heap in the spring.
My death will be by some other overpass
Most likely or maybe on some great bright bridge
Out in the open but not I hope in winter.

Heartbreak

The day Bobby Thomson hit that home run,
I played Bach on the piano.
My Dodger fan mother
burst into the living room,
angry at me, accusing. Perhaps I was at fault,
because I said I hated baseball,
or because I pretended, to annoy her,
that I liked the Giants
(though in fact I didn't know a double
from a double play). I knew better
than to pretend I liked the Yankees.

A week later, in the Series, she rooted for
the very Giants she had hated. I would
have said Go figure, but that phrase
was not in my vocabulary yet.

Now I read her diary and feel
what she was feeling.
"The Dodgers lost a heartbreaker today,
three-two." I imagine the voice
of Red Barber summering the air
as June sun yellows the drawn
linen shades. "It's a hah flah
ball," he says, "into raght field."
The fans go wild, I know not why.

Giamatti said baseball breaks your heart.
Brooklyn broke my mother's heart year in,
year out, and perhaps
her heart is stronger for it,
in all those broken places.

Night Mirror

No, not night exactly, the dusk
of night, and I am en route.
Their eyes are bright,
beasts' eyes in torchlight.
I flick the mirror up
into its dark night face.

Now dimmed, the eyes hover
in a false mist. Night
of the living dead Acuras,
the living dead Blazers. They
lurk, drop back, sidle to pass me
on our breakneck route,
a ghostly ride from the sleepy hollow
of home, or what passes for it,
into the brisk plain of day.
We are all ghosts,
neither here, in comfort,
nor there, in strait.

The others pull up, park
in the murk of day's break,
knowing that they will emerge
in daylight, maybe fading,
but daylight nonetheless.
I come out into bright afternoon
and find my life still
the tilted dark of a night mirror.

SCHEHERAZADE
For Mary N.

Something has gone wrong in the theatre of heaven.
The dark actor who plays the part of the Angel of Death
forgets his lines, addresses the wrong characters,
crosses off the wrong speeches in his prompt-book.
He wanders into the wrong set, selects the wrong names and faces
because they dwell near other, more likely candidates
to put on gowns made from white percale (Penney's white sale);
to strap on cardboard wings spangled with silver paper stars.
The ones selected are surprised; but they know their lines.
Not me! Already? There must be some mistake.

Meanwhile the casting director, who has too many responsibilities,
and who lunched too late and too heavily, has lost patience
with the actor in the dark hood and cloak.
These are the wrong names, he thunders.
*Look at this woman! Only forty-eight;
still in her prime. The one we wanted
is her neighbor, the sort we're used to.
We need someone with grandchildren,
who will give a fine funeral; most of all
we need someone who can bake, who knows
how to can peaches, how to cane chairs,
a sort of Renaissance woman who can conjugate Latin verbs
and diagram a sentence.* The actor is sullen, can say only
This one's an artiste. You'll see.
The lights in the echoing theatre darken
and the new candidate is brought out.

What can you offer us? I can dance a little.
She squints into the light; he is invisible.
Who taught you? I studied with Choura. She moves,
sways, executes some fouettés. The lilt is gone,
but her grace is there, her elegance, her line.
Her long gold hair comes down, sways in the dust
of the ancient theatre. The director leans forward.
Very nice. You were called in error. It was
your neighbor we wanted. Yes I know.
She pauses, finds that in this plane
she can hover in midair. I knew her well, she says.
Come down and tell me of her. She whispers in his ear.
It is like speaking into the whirlwind, but her fright is gone.
He smiles, the lights come up, a pearly dawn glows on the
    backdrop.

Ophelia Surfacing

Turning from side to side she mounts through lilies
Lifting her clear blind eyes to the unseen brightness;
Days in the dark have bleached her skin white as clamshells:
Hard pearls of cress stud her hair wound with tangled myrtle,
Clinging to ice-cold cheeks, dripping olive tendrils.

Where is the fennel now, where the rosemary
Bound with nettles and rue in her spicy garland:
Dark now and stinking of slime they are green still but rotting,
Rotting as she will rot when they finally lift her
Slippery oysterwhite limbs to be borne to charnel.

What did she find in the depths of that black bedchamber
Hung with thick bottlegreen curtains mottled with leeches,
What did her streaming eyes regard in the sunless
Aisle of the river bottom after her garments
Gave up their burden, letting her drop to the viscid
Carpet of slugs and leaves undisturbed by footprints?

Whom did she wed there, whose iron arms drew her under,
Whose glowing eyes held her gaze while her heartsblood
    bubbled,
Who pinned her down for that spasm of aqueous passion,
Why is she smiling, whose mouths are locked up forever,
Locked up with mud that dams the thick gush of pleasure?
We stand here gaping, astride on the sliding embankment,
Watching with thumbs in mouths as her gelid body,
Swollen and onion-shiny, is lifted skyward,
Untangled from ropes and weeds and dragged to the castle.

Exit, Pursued By A Bear

This is not the first time
I have been in this wood
but the last time
I knew where
I was
going.
This is
not the first time
I have
climbed
a tree
but the
last time
I was
dressed
for it.
Now I'm up here
I can see to the edge
of the forest. The green island
lapped by a yellow sea
of grain beyond, and even the cornflower
hills away to the bright west; perhaps the orchid
ocean as well with its cover of Prussian cloud.
The houses lining the northward road
seen from here are as square and true
and shiny as the picture tiles
round the fireplace of an early morning,
after the hearth has been swept and dried,
the tiles scrubbed and polished.
(The mildew and black rot,
the dead vines, the overgrown creepers,
the slops in the garden
invisible at this misty distance)
To think I passed through that tapestry
to get to this forest, to get to this place,
to my perch in this oak, heart pounding,
still brother to danger.
The bear must have found this view in the past
for he can climb too, and has joined me
on the next branch

Earthly Heaviness
(a triple poem)

Drop to earth in wind
      Scratch the air to find
   Swept away with breath
      Starpricks, pinholes, black
      In a cushion of white
Silkweed gathered in forty-two
To send for flotation.
      Sky a tiara for space
Body a silvery pod
      Pavé seen from the swamp
Crinkly lips whispering
Spreads apart, flies apart
   I'm landing! I'm landing!
      Miles apart, lightyears apart
Each sprout of silk bursts away
Floating to catch on loosestrife
      Flickering dust in the nighttime
      Coalstars caught on threads of aurora
Pips sunk in mud
White fingers gravid
      Glints set in the teeth of planets.
Mulch brings up branches
That fight with the wind.
      Light shoots straight down
      Through the coreholes of your eyes
      To the planted soles of your feet.

Rosy

New sunglasses make things rosy. Liquid peach
fills up the marble lobby, making pink
the faces of the clerks. Their motions cease.
For a tiny flash they are cerise,
light chunks of fruit inside a jelly mold
served at a church picnic in midsummer: cool
thoughts while gazing through the doors at noon
downtown in August. Sunglasses make the city rosy.
Sidewalks flat as salmon glow
in shimmering champagne light.
                    Remember when
you felt the rush of air before the first
cyclone of summer and breathed deep.
Rejoice in that fresh draught, rejoice in sky
pale as an opened lime, rejoice to see
the sun reblossom in the trees,
rosy, made rosier still
by tinted lenses. Even in the rain
just fallen, standing by the tumbled crates
beneath the awning, you saw how the pears
still green yet glowed. Rosy, like the ramblers
on the ragged fence. It is
the only way to see.

Mars Over Bowen Road

Worlds are unreal on buses
at six-thirty in the morning.
My ears are full of Mozart and my eye
strays from Descartes. Outside the fixed
smeared pane a field slides past.
Over it, surely not real, a shell we call
the moon, sandy with equinoctial mist. Beneath,
a pink marble known as Mars. The greening sky
could be a lawn, and these two globes
could be a final out in that old game
I'd thought forgotten. My pen falls from my hand
and I neglect for now the French philosopher.
I feel the driveway grit scrape my bare knees.
We used a stick to draw the circle and the lines,
and now it's my turn. I hold the chipped blue agate
(the one that brings me luck) between the arch
of my index finger, flick my thumb
and watch the missile spin
across a tiny universe of white
and green and piebald glass. We are such stuff
that never loses moments of small glee,
of unimportant triumph; and our days
are flights as dreams are made on, full of time,
of clocks to march the time, of lonely
leaf-strewn corners where we wait
for buses in the dawn; and our little lives,
striving with Herrick and Flaubert to block
the pain of wasted hours, are full of
games and rounded with pure sleep.

First Moonset

We were promised snow,
but instead we have moon,
a flat gold plate on the rail
of the black December horizon.

I watch it from the window;
the bus carries me along with it.
Branches make striations
across its flat face.

How high is it? I cannot measure,
except with my eyes, but know
that as the opposite sky
brightens its gold will fade.

We have been tricked into this
gazing and worshipping,
believing down the years
that this night's sun is
as powerful as the other.

Rescued from this folly years ago,
now we observe the moon as rock,
see that its light casts no prism,
know that it is slave, as are we,
to the real sun's comings and goings.

We have even ventured out to it,
crawled like grubs on its cold surface,
seen ourselves as it sees us
--if it could see--but still
it compels us, with its

risings, its blood and silver,
its spangling in lakes, its
waxing and waning, its monthly sulks.
Our minds have turned this cold reject
of earth into a dream of earth itself,
making me wonder how many
errors we are capable of,
or how strong nature is
to outlast us all.

Moon While Tossing Out Mouse

The cat caught a mouse
last night so I came out
to toss the victim in the bushes.
I look up. The moon rests
bright in the branches,
the sky dark, not black yet.
I don't know you,
I've watched you and watched
and written about you, thought I
knew you but you changed.
I must learn again.
It is hard to comprehend
this coin in the cup of sky.

If I stood on your surface
bald landscape would stretch
more miles than I could walk;
there would be no bush
to throw this mouse into,
no trees to peer through
at a gibbous earth. In place of
the white Cape next door
would be a hard hill of stone,
and dust would mold my steps.

Sky would be gone, and in its space
nothing. Earth is a rage, an overburden
of life, all sizes. The dead mouse, flying
through the air to its resting place
will generate life, but you
generate nothing. No wonder
you pass the sun's light
to us; it's all you can do,
your only trick,
and it enthralls us.

FIRE

At first we used kerosene,
stopping on hot July tarmac to fill
our rusty can at the BP station
in case the general store out in the Ontario
bush didn't have any. The fires it made
bloomed for a moment, scented the green air
with city fumes, then drooped and faded,
tiger lilies in a glass jar.

Then we discovered birchbark,
gathering zebra-striped sheaves, husbanded
like sugar or coffee. From a fallen
birch on an unnamed island in the Restoule
River we cut rubbery rolls of moldy
bark and bundled them, dank diplomas
in the bow of the canoe.

Better still were the fir cones
smacking down on the beaches in hot wind.
We filled our caps with them. Sticky wombs
of fire, they bore dense flames, coral-dark,
bleeding thick heat on the ashy bed
of yesterday's campfires.

Brushing through the cool hanging fragrance
of witchhazel bushes at the water's edge,
we leave the boat to climb the mountain, a great
quartzite rock rising out of the cold lake.
We reach the nearest top of the world, to stand
in orange light to see, dark as stoats,
islands in Georgian Bay.
If we stayed up here a little longer
our fires would light themselves, we would bear
light down with us, in our eyes, in our hands.

Stories

by

Mary Ann Eichelberger

Mother's Candy Jar

Ruth left the cemetery before the final graveside prayers because she didn't want to witness the priest sprinkling holy water on her father's coffin, thinking it was a dirty trick they had played on the old man, giving him a Catholic burial when he had never set foot in a Catholic church and most of his life had scoffed at the idea of a God and had begun to waver only after his last illness when he faced death with a terror that burned black in his foggy blue eyes.

She had no idea what he had said to her brothers and sister; she only knew what he said to her, and what he said was: "When I go I want a minister to say a few prayers at the funeral home, then I just want to go in the ground next to your mother. You can get a minister, you have Lutheran friends, you can get one to come. I was baptized a Lutheran and I want to be buried a Lutheran. I know I never went to church, but I got to have something when I die, and that's what I want. There, now I said it and you know it. You tell the others."

She did tell them, but when they said they were going to give him a Catholic burial, complete with a Mass, she didn't argue, they were so determined to do it their way. With cold accusing eyes they dared her to challenge them, but were careful not to glance her way when, acting as the spokesman, her oldest brother convinced the priest that it was their father's wish. Her heart was a cold lump in her chest when the bronze coffin was wheeled down the center aisle of St. Martin's Church.

You reach a point, she thought, after fleeing the cemetery and driving into her garage, when you just don't want to be contradicted and criticized anymore, when you just don't care enough to defend one more time what you know to be the truth. In the end, what difference did it make who presided over his burial? He was still going into the ground. A little holy water sprinkled over his coffin would not change a thing, but she didn't have to watch the cold tears of her siblings dribbling on to the coffin top, intermingling with the holy water, and hear people murmur afterwards: "Howard/Ernest/Grace took it real hard." And they might not say it, but it would be written all over their faces: "Ruth's hard, always was, she had a good husband, he gave her everything, look at that big house she lives in, the fancy car, she must have gotten plenty from him when she sent him packing, must have taken him to the cleaners, Ruth's hard."

When she came into her kitchen she saw that the answering machine by the telephone was flashing. There were messages from her son and daughter. They had offered to come to the funeral, but she had dissuaded them. What good would they be to their grandfather now? They had both visited him last summer. She didn't need them to help her through the funeral. As far as she was concerned, her father, the father she had known in younger days, had died years ago, had left a shriveled skeleton to shuffle from chair to chair, to pick at his food and glare at her, red with anger, because she could not get him relief from constant pain and confusion, because she took his car keys and forced him to sell his '78 Buick.

"You'll kill somebody some day if you keep on driving when you can't see well, you're almost deaf, you just can't drive anymore," she told him two weeks after his ninety-second birthday.

"You had a lot of nerve taking his car keys, forcing him to sell his car," Grace said. "And what I'd like to see is the receipt, see if he got that money in the bank. That's what I'd like to see, who got the money, you were so determined to get rid of his car."

"I don't know what he did with the receipt," Ruth said, getting mean pleasure from the sight of her sister's face, the pursed lips, narrowed eyes, the cords in her neck tightening like fat strings. "Ask him." She had driven her father to the bank to make the deposit, but, she thought, "If Grace wants to think I did something underhanded, let her, she's going to think wrong of me anyway, no matter what proof I give her."

Howard and Ernest and Grace, when they came to visit, insisted too heartily that he "looked good". Grace, who always brought a pie or a cake, would remark, "What an appetite Father has, did you see him dig into that coconut cake? Last night I made meat loaf and he ate two helpings and finished the mashed potatoes, scraping the dish until Bert and I laughed and I asked him, Father, don't you get any good food unless I come to cook for you? It made Bert and me feel good to see him polish his plate like he did, although I said to Bert after Father went to bed, I wonder what he eats when we're not here, when he runs out of things I bring. Poor thing."

Ruth brought her father meals to warm in his microwave, she picked him up every Sunday and brought him to her home for dinner, she talked to him on the phone or went to see him every day, things Grace, who lived ninety miles away, chose not to acknowledge as she chattered on and on about "how good it is to see Father dig into the food I cook for him."

Grace stocked his freezer with homemade dinners she had brought in an ice chest, taped cooking instructions on each one, scrubbed the kitchen floor and left three days later glowing from good deeds accomplished, especially from pointing out to Ruth, the resident caregiver, all the things that Ruth did wrong in dealing with their father.

"You make him mad when you remind him to take his pill, you know he hates to be treated like a child, he's as sharp as a tack, he doesn't need reminding, you ought to treat him more like I do, like he wants to be treated, my goodness if I were him I'd snap at you, too, the way you remind him that he has a doctor's appointment, as if he'd forget, he's on top of things, you'd have to get up pretty early in the morning to put one over on him. He's just a marvel, no trouble at all."

Ruth wondered, didn't her sister notice that their father frequently slept in his clothes, that he wore the same underwear for days, that he stock piled spoiled food in the back of his refrigerator, that sometimes he forgot that his wife was dead?

Grace repeated it so often that Ruth got dizzy listening, "Father's just great, no trouble, no trouble at all. He's sharp, so sharp."

But once when Ruth didn't feel well and asked her sister to stay over a day to take the old man to the urologist, Grace came up with a litany of excuses, "You know I'd love to, but I have to get home and anyway you know more about his doctors than I do and besides Father's more comfortable with you. What do you think is wrong with you? You look fine to me, maybe you ate too much of that rhubarb cobbler I brought, you know I don't think you eat good unless I bring food for Father and you dig in, probably eat too much, it tastes so good to you. There's nothing wrong with you. I can't stay longer. It's out of the question and, anyway, Father is used to you taking him to the doctor's."

It seemed their father was better off with Ruth when it was time to sit for hours in doctor's offices, or in hospitals, or at the druggist waiting for a prescription that he often refused to pay for when he looked at the price.

But Grace did more than Howard and Ernest who, since their mother's death, dreaded visiting, and who, when they came, dragged the old man, despite his aching bones, all over the country side in their cars, counting the minutes until their "duty visits" were over for another year.

Her brothers did not bring food in coolers. They took their father to restaurants and let him pay the check. When they left for home they usually managed to get something in the car that they thought their father didn't need anymore, like the marble- topped table that had been in the family for generations and the grandfather clock that Howard got in his station wagon. He said he would get it fixed, and probably he did, but he never brought it back to its place in the dusty front hall.

"That clock should be mine, I'm the oldest," he said once, although she had never asked him.

There was nothing in the house that she wanted.

Except the candy jar.

But they all wanted that.

Because of their mother. She had always kept it filled with sour balls and red and white peppermints wrapped in cellophane and Milky Ways and packages of peanut M & M's. It was kept on the dining room buffet. It wasn't valuable, just a tall footed jar with etchings of butterflies and flowers and a cover that made a sound of glass on glass when you replaced it, alerting the rest of the family.

"Who's in the candy jar?" they would yell, and the culprit wouldn't have to confess, his or her cheeks would be bulging with the stolen treat. Part of the fun, their mother always said, was "to sneak a piece out of the jar." She had only one rule: the last piece could not be taken by anyone except their father. But the jar was never that close to being empty until after the day their father found their mother at the bottom of the broken rotting cellar stairs that he had said he would fix when he was "damn good and ready."

"Where did the candy jar come from in the first place?" Ruth asked when she was a little girl.

"Your Aunt Vi got it when she worked in Wick's candy store before she got married," her mother said. "There was a matching bowl that got broken, but I don't remember how. Maybe it just slipped out of somebody's hands, maybe it was your grandma. Vi gave me the jar filled with jelly beans when you kids were little. It was just something they sold at the candy store."

The candy jar, always full, was like Mother, who had been full of love for each and every one of them. Keeping the candy jar full was one of the proofs of her love. It was as comforting as the smell of cinnamon rolls fresh from the oven, bed sheets straight from the drying line in the yard.

Her father said, when he was asked about the jar, "When I'm gone you can decide among yourselves who gets it. I'm not going to say and pick one so the other three of you will be mad at me."

Once, when he was in the hospital with a broken arm, his bones so brittle that the arm had to be set with pins, he whispered to Ruth, "Get the jar. Keep it. You deserve it, you're the best to me. Always have been." She choked back tears, not because he was so frail, tubes dripping nutrients into his body and another tube draining urine out, not because he was offering her the coveted jar, but because she knew that he did appreciate all she had done for him, but also knew he would never tell the others. All his life he had been a man afraid to take a stand. A Lutheran, he had married her mother in the rectory of St. Martin's church, had watched his children grow up in a religion he did not believe in, and had never had the courage to speak out. Now he would not speak out about the jar. Not even for her, who wiped the drool from his chin and brought him rice pudding with raisins and whipped cream in a Waterford bowl.

When she left that night he did not want to let go of her hand. With closed eyes, he whispered again, "Remember, it's yours, the candy jar is yours."

When she mentioned it to her younger brother he said, "Father told me the jar was mine."

"You know what I think?" she said."I think he told each of us the same thing."

Ernest laughed."I'll toss a coin with you, heads it's mine, tails it's yours."

She shook her head. "I don't want to lose."

"It's just a jar," he said.

"Then why do you want it?" she asked.

"Probably for the same reason you do," he said.

They didn't say it, but each of them wanted the jar as some kind of a victory over the others. It was like when they were little, vying for their mother's affection.

Now, wanting to get the image of her father's grave out of her mind, Ruth made a cup of tea and carried it to the table in the family room. She sat and looked out at the red and yellow leaves scuttling across the lawn and thought: "This winter I won't have to worry about him freezing because he turned the heat off. I won't have to drive him to the doctor's in a snow storm."

She remembered last January when she found him at his kitchen table with the furnace turned off. Layered in sweaters, two pairs of dirty socks and worn slippers on his feet, food crusted on the table and the floor because he wouldn't allow a cleaning woman in, he sat hunched in pain, surrounded by piles of papers he said he was "sorting through."

"Dad, I'm going to turn the furnace on, it's freezing in the house, your bed room is like a refrigerator, the floor feels like ice," she said.

He glowered from under bushy white brows, his jaw shaking. "You leave your hands off my furnace, you don't pay my heating bills."

"I'll pay your heat bill, it's not like you're down to your last penny, but I'll pay it and I'm going to turn the furnace on," she said.

"Go ahead !" he shouted. "And soon as you're gone I'll turn it off, see how you like that, this isn't your house."

He lurched forward, then fell back, groaning and she knew at once that he had broken one of the bones in his back again. He finally admitted he had lifted piles of wood in the yard and had injured his back. It hurt to move and he could walk only with great pain, but when she tried to call an ambulance and the doctor he shook his fist at her, shouting, "I won't get in the ambulance if it does come. I'm not going to the hospital, nobody can make me. You can't tell me what to do."

She went to the corner drugstore and used a pay phone to call her oldest brother. He lived a five hour drive away, but he was retired and she thought if he came maybe he could convince their father that he needed medical attention, that he needed to heat the house. Her sister-in-law answered the phone.

"You interrupted our afternoon prayers, Ruth. What do you want with Howard?" Mae asked. "What ever it is, you can tell me, he is saying his afternoon prayers, he gets very annoyed if he is interrupted, you should know that, then we both read from the Bible, we shouldn't be interrupted, this is our time with God."

Ruth stifled a snort of contempt, knowing that when they were through praying and reading the Bible they would treat themselves to a double manhattan and a bowl of cashews and get sloshed in a most pious way. She said, "Dad's in pain, he hurt his back, he won't let me turn the heat on and it's ten degrees outside, the house is freezing, I thought if Howard came maybe he could help me get Dad to listen to reason. He needs to go to the hospital."

"You can't expect us to drop everything and drive all that way just because you don't know how to handle your own father," Mae said. "We were just there a few months ago, he was wonderful with us. Really, Ruth, I don't think you know how to handle him, just go back and try to be nicer to him. See if he'll take some aspirin. He's never been any trouble for us. And another thing, why do you always call him Dad when the rest of us call him Father? You always have to make yourself different, don't you? Maybe it's because you think you are better, writing all that poetry and stuff and I have to tell you, you'd be better off using your energy praying the way Howard and I do. God is the only truth, Ruth."

Next Ruth tried her sister, but Grace was too "upset" to listen to her and said, "Why can't you be nicer to Father so that he'll cooperate with you? Anyway, it's his house, if he wants to turn the furnace off, that's his business." She turned the phone over to her husband who accused Ruth of upsetting her sister. "Now," Bert whined, "she'll get a headache, she's crying. If your Father wants to turn off the heat that's his business."

"Bert," Ruth said, "I just want to know, will you come and help me get him to a doctor?"

"You're making a big fuss over nothing," he said."Your sister is too upset–"

"Goodbye, Bert," she said and hung up.

Two days later her father broke down and admitted he needed help. Exhausted and worried, she had him brought to the hospital by ambulance. He was suffering from hypothermia and dehydration. In the emergency room, he clung to her hand, his eyes scared, but when she bent over him to comfort him, she suddenly remembered her mother at the bottom of the cellar steps he had refused to fix and she had a hard time feeling any pity for him until he was wheeled into an examining room and she heard him scream with pain as he was lifted from the gurney.

That was when she knew she could not take care of him any more. She went into the chapel and asked God to keep her from becoming bitter and to help her to forgive Howard and Grace for refusing to believe her, to help her, to help their aged father.

She called Ernest and he came as soon as he could get a flight out of Dallas. They put the old man in a nursing home. He died the day after he signed the papers for the sale of his house and she knew it was because he had finally given up because, with the house gone, he knew he could never go home again.

Ruth drank her tea and waited for the telephone to ring. It would be Ernest. He had always been her favorite. Last night, when they had sat with the lawyer reading their father's will, he had been the only one who had not been outraged when she said she was renouncing her share of their father's estate in favor of her daughter and son.

"Your kids have had everything handed to them on a silver platter, why should they get Father's money?" Grace demanded. "If you have so much that you don't want it, I think you should divide it among the three of us."

"Give some of it to the church," Howard said. "Your children have already had too many worldly things, why should they get Father's money? It will ruin them. You always spoiled them."

She didn't defend either her intentions or her children, although she bit back the words: "My children never got arrested for possession of drugs, for stealing a car, for drunk driving like yours did."

Ernest said, "Ruth can do what she wants." He sat next to her in the shabby living room. His wife had not come for the funeral because she was taking care of their grandson.

Grace snapped, "She always does exactly as she pleases, ask her why she threw her husband out, he was always so good to her, if he did have that one little fling with his secretary it was only because Ruth was so mean to him, going away to those poetry things instead of taking care of him, he had needs, you know, and he had money and she took plenty when she divorced him. And as for your poetry, Ruth," she glared at her, "I don't understand it, my friends and I laugh at it, it's so dumb."

"Maybe you're dumb and that's why you don't understand it," Ruth said. She got up and put on her sweater. "I'll see you in church tomorrow morning."

Grace tried to get in the parting shot, "It'll probably be the first time in years that you've been in church."

"I go to church about as often as your children do, Grace, "Ruth said, enjoying her sister's discomfiture at hearing the truth spoken. She squeezed Ernest's shoulder on her way out and kissed the top of his balding gray head. She knew he wanted to be with her, but that he didn't have the gumption to get up and walk out with her. He knew she would always forgive him, the others would not.

The telephone rang and for a second Ruth thought she would not answer it because she knew what they wanted and she knew she would never tell them, not even Ernest. After this day she would not see Howard and Grace again, the anger and bitterness between them a thick wall that she, for one, did not care to scale. Let them stay on their side of the world and she would stay on hers.

She picked up the receiver.

"Are you going to come over?" Ernest asked. She could feel Howard and Mae and Grace and Bert straining to hear what was being said, trying to figure out what she would do, if Ernest could persuade her to come back to their father's house.

"No."

"Well–Ruth, is there nothing you want that's here? Not a table, or a picture, or something?"

"Nothing."

"Well–we were wondering–do you know where the candy jar is?"

"Isn't it on the buffet?"

"No. Do you know where it is?"

"You know as well as I do that it was always kept on the buffet."

"But it's not there now and nobody has seen it."

"You have been at the house, one of you should know where it is," Ruth said. She could hear Grace hissing in the background, "She took it, I know she did, who else had the opportunity? And what I'd like to know is what else she might have walked off with. Ask her that while you're at it, ask her that ."

"We thought you would know where it is," Ernest said.

"Look around, maybe you'll find it."

His voice was tight. "Okay, Ruth. I'll say goodbye then. I wish you would have come over to be with us after the funeral, but I think

I understand. I hope you get to Dallas one of these days."

She hung up, smiling. Let them bicker over what remained of their father's things, let them search the house for the candy jar, let them suspect for the rest of their lives that she had taken it, they would never know. Because the secret was hers. The night after her father died she drove to his house to get his dark gray suit for his burial. On her way past the buffet she picked up the empty candy jar and took it home. She rolled it in bubble wrap and brown paper, tied it with twine and put it on a kitchen shelf until that morning, an hour before the funeral, when she drove to the cemetery.

She stood at the edge of the open grave, looking down into the muddy bottom where soon the coffin holding her father's body would be lowered and she said, "Dad, you never could say who could have the candy jar, so you keep it."

She held it over the grave, then let go. It made a splashing sound as it hit bottom and settled into the mud.

After The Storm

Saturday, when the snow first began to fall, Dorothea hurried to the supermarket to stock up on eggs and milk as well as cheese and crackers and frozen shrimp for Jack in case they couldn't get out on their regular Saturday night date. Driving home she imagined a romantic evening before the fire with her lover. There was no room in her fantasy for her mother, who was in the habit of sitting in the living room watching TV until after the eleven o'clock news.

It was her mother, of course, who predicted the blizzard would make driving impossible. All afternoon she maintained her vigil by the kitchen window. She said, "Jack won't get out tonight. The storm is not letting up."

Dorothea, who had heard the latest weather report on the radio, agreed. "We're in for at least another day of this."

When Jack called, she tantalized him with the frozen shrimp and the bottle of champagne chilling in the refrigerator. "Why don't you save all those goodies and maybe I can get over tomorrow," Jack said.

Dorothea was stunned. For twenty-five years they had gone out every Saturday, but they seldom saw one another on a Sunday. It was not considered a "date day" for them. He promised to call back later that night. They both laughed when she said they would finally get to watch the BritComs on PBS.

Irene was delighted to have her daughter's company on a Saturday evening. She never mentioned it, but she was resentful that Dorothea went out every Saturday night while she was left alone with a cold supper and the TV for company. She did not think Dorothea was as considerate of her mother's feelings as she should be.

The two women prepared supper together while they listened to the storm bulletins on the kitchen radio. They had Campbell's tomato soup and grilled cheese sandwiches with pickles and olives. Dorothea tried not to think of the broiled lamb chops or the thick slab of prime ribs of beef she would have feasted on had she gone to dinner with Jack. Later, watching the escapades of lovers on an old movie, she tried not to think about how she and Jack made love on the couch every Saturday night while her mother was safely asleep.

Sunday morning Dorothea awakened hoping for the sound of the plows, but all she heard was the shrieking winds of the blizzard. At breakfast her mother announced that the weather forecast called for high winds and more snow for at least another twenty-four hours.

"Jack won't get through today," Irene said, spreading orange marmalade on her whole wheat toast.

Dorothea sighed, "Well, this might be a good time for me to clean out my closet. Get rid of some things I never wear anymore."

Irene jumped in. "Like that gold sweater. It makes you look so sallow!"

Dorothea decided to let that remark pass; after all, her mother was getting up in years, she couldn't be expected to be tactful about everything. She decided, however, to keep the gold sweater. She also decided, when Jack called an hour later, to take his call in her bedroom with the door firmly shut.

"My street is all plowed out," he told her. "Call me the minute they get to you and I'll be over in ten minutes!"

"Oh, Jack," she moaned, "you know they never get to my street until last."

He said, "It might not be a good idea for me to leave Mother. She is so nervous in a storm. I do miss you, dear. Last night was so lonely without you."

His concern for his mother made her more concerned for her own as she went through her closet, putting clothes in bags for the Salvation Army. She decided they would have their own little party that evening. It would cheer them both up. She cooked the shrimp in a curry sauce. She set out crackers and cheese. She lit the fire. She popped the cork on the champagne.

Outside snow pelted the windows, winds ripped branches from the maple trees and dashed them to the ground, but there were no sounds of traffic and that silence was louder than the storm.

"If there was an emergency how would the fire engines or the ambulance get through?" Irene asked.

"I doubt there will be an emergency," Dorothea said.

"I could have a heart attack," Irene fretted. "Or there could be a fire in the chimney. You could have appendicitis. You know, the doctor thought you had that once when you were ten years old. You never know, it could be acute next time."

Dorothea laughed. "Don't think about things like that. It's nice by the fire. Let's enjoy it."

"We didn't get to church today, the paper boy didn't come, I didn't make a roast for dinner, what kind of a Sunday is this?" Irene demanded. In the wing chair by the fireplace she looked shrunken and old, her shoulders hunched in a navy cardigan.

"Why don't we just be grateful that we have this lovely home to be safe in, that we have this nice warm fire and champagne and good things to eat," Dorothea said.

"I suppose you miss your boyfriend," Irene said.

Dorothea answered, "It's nice being with you."

But her mother screwed up her face in disbelief. "I never understood why you two didn't get married."

Dorothea stared at her mother's flushed face. Was it possible that Irene did not know that she had never married Jack because they had never been able to figure out how they could marry and set up their own household while helping their mothers maintain their own. Besides, they had always been content with their lives the way they were. Dorothea liked her job at the bank, the orderliness of her existence. She liked living with her mother. Jack was happy with his life. He enjoyed his job at an insurance company. They met three times a week for lunch, went out to dinner every Wednesday and Saturday night. Once a year they took a vacation together, although they told their mothers and friends that she was going to visit a girlfriend and he was attending an insurance convention.

Irene nibbled a piece of cheese, not really expecting an answer, satisfied with the shocked expression on her daughter's face. She, too, liked her life the way it was and certainly did not want Dorothea to marry and desert her and she most definitely did not want Jack moving into her home; having a man around would upset the delicate balance of their lives.

Irene's question went unanswered. Dorothea thought it was an issue better off left unexplored. Irene finally brought up what was really bothering her. "Wouldn't you think one of the boys would call to see how we are making out in this storm? It's been on all the news channels. There is no way Ed and Bob don't know we've been buried by this blizzard."

Dorothea had long ago given up on her brothers showing more than a casual interest in the welfare of her mother and herself. She couldn't understand why her mother couldn't get it through her head that neither Ed nor Bob would call. It never occurred to her that Irene was jealous of Jack's attention and concern and yearned to have someone special of her own.

The next morning Jack called to say he could walk to the corner and catch a bus to work. He advised Dorothea to stay put. "You don't want to risk being stranded in this weather," he said. "Besides, if you couldn't get home, think about your mother."

Dorothea promised Jack she would not attempt to walk her unplowed street to the bus, agreeing with him that her mother would be frantic. Looking out the window at the drifting snow and the unplowed street she felt like a prisoner with little hope of a parole. She ached for the sight of Jack, for his touch, for the sound of his voice.

"Let's play gin rummy," her mother suggested.

It was better than staring at TV, but Dorothea went nuts over her mother's habit of drumming her fingers on the table top. She sent short desperate prayers heavenward that at least one of her brothers would call and satisfy her mother's need to have them care. The day dragged by until it was dinner time and the two women could not decide what they wanted to eat. Exasperated, Dorothea made an omelet which she divided sloppily and dumped onto plates which, her mother pointed out, she had neglected to warm. Dorothea filled the frying pan with cold water.

"I wish you wouldn't do that, Dorothea. Putting cold water into a hot pan is very, very bad," Irene scolded.

Dorothea defended her action belligerently. "I always do that."

"I don't know where you picked up such a bad habit. I never do that," Irene protested. Actually, having her daughter home the last few days made Irene aware that there were many things about Dorothea that were irritating. Like her habit of not making her bed before breakfast. Also she walked restlessly from one room to another, picking up a book or a magazine and discarding it wherever she happened to be, getting in Irene's way as she went about her daily puttering.

They ate their omelet in sullen silence.

Jack called punctually at nine o'clock. Dorothea was short with him, envious that he was able to get out of the house while she would be stuck with her mother for at least another day. She had no idea that her mother longed to have the house to herself, longed to be able to watch her soap operas without snide remarks from her daughter, longed to have her kitchen tidy.

The two women who had lived in harmony most of their lives were suddenly in discord because the snow storm had interrupted their routine. They strained for the sounds of the plows and spent hours staring out the windows, listening to the weather reports on the radio.

On the morning of the fourth day they awakened to the roar of the plow bulldozing its way down the street. Dorothea wasted no time in calling the boy down the street to use his snowblower on their driveway. Still in her nightgown and robe she dashed to the telephone to call Jack, ignoring her mother's sarcastic remarks: "He'll think you can't think of anything else but seeing him. And in your nightgown yet."

Jack was ecstatic to learn that her street had been plowed. He promised to come over after dinner.

Dorothea shampooed her hair and dressed carefully that evening in the blue wool dress she had bought for last Saturday's date. After dinner she sat with her mother in the living room, both of them listening for the sound of Jack's car, Dorothea

After The Storm   Mary Ann Eichelberger

wondering how she could tactfully ask her mother to leave her alone with her lover. Irene, like an animal licking its wounds, was trying not to show the hurt she felt that neither of her sons had called. Bob lived in Texas and perhaps they didn't print the news about the Buffalo blizzard. Ed lived in Detroit and maybe he was too worried about selling cars to think about his mother. But–still–what would it take to call their mother? Was it impossible for either of them to realize that a call from them brightened her life for weeks? She envied her daughter. At least Dorothea had something to look forward to. Dorothea had Jack and Irene had nobody. Jealousy made her angry and resentful.

    Mother and daughter jumped at the sound of a car door slamming. Dorothea put a hand to her hair to smooth any stray strands, unaware of her mother's icy scrutiny.

    "I'll just stay a few minutes to say hello to Jack," Irene promised, and then, to her horror, heard herself add, "Don't worry, I'll leave the two of you to the couch."

    Dorothea froze on the way to the door to admit her lover. The blood pounded in her ears. A strangled gasp croaked from her throat.

    Then, intoxicated by her power, Irene continued triumphantly. "I always hear you come home, tiptoe to my room to see if I'm asleep. Do you think I am so old, been widowed so long that I forgot the sounds of making love? The groans, the moans, the thumps–"

    "Stop it!" Dorothea shouted, swaying with anger and humiliation. She wanted to turn around and slap her mother. Jack's footsteps came up the steps. Trembling she opened the door.

    He embraced her, kissing her forehead gently. "Why, darling, you're shaking."

    "She's so thrilled to see you," Irene grinned, her upper plate slipping with a click. She did not sit down, but stood in the archway for a few minutes, inquiring about his mother before she said, "I'm sure you two will want to be alone. I'll go into the kitchen and do some mending."

    Jack moved closer to Dorothea on the couch, putting his arms around her, hugging her tight. "Poor little girl, was it dreadful for you? Thank God that terrible storm is over."

"It isn't over," she muttered. She was not referring to the blizzard, but to the raging emotions her mother had stirred up. There could be only one reason why Irene had revealed that she had known all these years about the lovemaking on the couch: to let Dorothea know she had not gotten away with it, to reduce her to the status of a naughty child being caught in the act.

"Of course it's over, darling," he insisted. "You've just got a bad case of the old cabin fever."

"No, it's not that, sweetheart, it's just that these last few days made me realize something," she said, her mind made up.

"What's that?"

"Jack," she said, smiling, knowing there was one sure way to get even with her mother, "I think it's time we got married."

THE BROKEN BOWL

All Saturday morning the blizzard warnings continued over the radio as Beryl packed Wally's things in cardboard cartons from the supermarket. As she folded and tucked in corners, she listened for the sound of his Volkswagen chugging up the gravel driveway.

She was resigned to his leaving, although it had been devastating at first to suspect that he had found someone else. Some nights he did not come home and he never bothered to call, just showed up the next morning for clean clothes. In a temper one morning he blurted out the truth.

She had asked him why he always said he was working late when she knew that was not the case. After all, she always called his office (not to check, as he accused, but to find out if she should make him a late dinner) and he was never there.

"You drive me nuts," Wally raged. "You're on me every minute of the day. You can never leave me alone for a lousy minute. Okay, if you want to know, there is someone else."

"Who is she?" Beryl demanded.

"It's Judy."

Judy! One of their friends from the crowd they hung around with. Judy was short, plump, had frizzy red hair and long green eyes. She rarely moved, but sat in one spot, curled up like a purring cat. She had been paired off with Barney ever since Beryl could remember. "What about Barney?" she asked.

"Who cares," Wally said, anxious, now that it was out in the open, to make a speedy exit. "I'll pick up my things in a few days."

That was more than a week ago. Night after night she came home and searched the house for evidence that he had come during her absence. He never had, and so she washed his dirty clothes, ironed his shirts, took his suit to the cleaners and worked at getting used to being without him. Finally, that morning, she called and told him to come for his things. He protested that a major storm was forecast, but she stood her ground. He had, she reminded him, driven in worse weather and, if he hurried, he could get there and back before the storm got really bad. She didn't tell him that she wanted all of his stuff out of the house as final proof that they were through.

Finished with the packing, Beryl checked the wood supply in the back room, then, dressed in her parka and boots, trudged out to the barn with a canvas sling. First, battling the wind, she filled the bird feeders and hung suet cakes on the trees. The snow drifted into a high pile across her path as she made several trips back and forth with her sling filled with enough logs to keep the house cozy for a few days. Back inside the kitchen she stamped snow off her feet and blew on her frozen fingers, unaware that Wally had come in through the front door and stood glaring at her, dripping snow onto the rug.

"Where's all this stuff you're so anxious to get rid of that I had to rush out in the middle of the blizzard?" he demanded.

Beryl gazed upon the disgruntled face of her beloved, heart lurching because he looked so cold and miserable. "I didn't hear you come in. I thought you'd come to the back door. I went out to bring in more wood. You know how I am, always prepared, that's my motto."

He kicked off his boots. "I didn't want my car to get stuck in those drifts in the back. All the roads are getting bad. I want to get going as soon as possible."

He walked to the back window. "It's so damn desolate here, like living in Siberia. I'll never know why you had to buy this God-forsaken dump."

She knew why she had wanted to move to this old farm house. It was because in the country, away from the bustle of the city, she had thought she could have him all to herself. She had dreamed of intimate dinners before the fireplace on winter evenings, of long, lazy weekends reading and going for hikes in the woods, of a life together of love and contentment. It was her romantic soul that had made her happy to turn the old farm house into a haven for them.

"You're leaving it now, there's no reason to carry on about it," she said.

He shed his coat and hat and held his hands out to the fireplace. She bolted the back door against the howling wind.

"Judy didn't want me to come out here," he said.

"Because of the storm?"

"Yeah, that, but she didn't want me to see you." He watched her, rubbing one foot over the top of the other.

"Then I guess you'd better hurry back," she said, astonished at the lightness of her tone when her heart was so heavy.

"I'm starved. I didn't have any breakfast and it must be lunch time already." He almost asked her for lunch. He knew he wouldn't have to go all the way. He knew she would take care of his needs, even though he had broken her heart.

"I can give you some soup," she said.

"Vegetable soup?"

"That's what's on the stove. And fresh rolls I made this morning." She stood at the kitchen door.

"Whole wheat, I suppose," he sniffed.

"Yes, whole wheat."

"Well–that vegetable soup is kinda good. Are the rolls those crusty ones?"

"Yes."

"Okay, you can give me some lunch. I'd better eat something before I head back into the city." Wally made it sound as if he were doing her a favor by letting her feed him. He flopped in his chair by the fire, stretching his toes to catch the warmth.

In her haste, her eagerness to give him nourishing food, Beryl dropped a blue willow bowl. It shattered on the yellow vinyl floor. It was a favorite, one she had picked up at an antique store. She was sad as she swept it up. It was silly to get attached to a bowl, but she felt the shattering of the bowl was symbolic of the shattering of her relationship with Wally. She had loved him, cared for him, worried over him, supported him, and he left her, not caring that her heart was in as many pieces as the broken bowl.

"Hey, what's taking so long?" Wally called. "The snow is piling up out there. I have to get out of here and get home."

Home! It hurt to hear him call someplace else home. Outside the kitchen window snow was accumulating in a huge drift. She said, "The plower should be here soon, Wally. It might be better to wait for him to clear the road than to start out right away. You could get stuck."

"Only you would find a house with a driveway two miles long," he sneered.

"It's hardly that long," she protested, bringing in his lunch tray.

"It seems that long. It's so damn isolated here. How can you bear living out here all by yourself?" he asked.

She replied, "I didn't know I'd be living here all alone."

"Aw, don't start," he objected, setting the tray across the arms of his chair. "Can't I eat my lunch in peace?"

"I wasn't going to start anything," she said, sitting on the floor, legs crossed, listening to her beloved slurping his soup.

He looked around the room. "What's in those boxes, Beryl? I didn't think I had so many clothes and things."

"Things add up. Everything is clean. I ironed your shirts," she said, wondering if he could possibly know that she had been happy to do these things for him.

"You're the limit," he said. "What other woman would do a guy's laundry after he dumped her for another dame? Jeez–you know–that's really the problem with you, Beryl–you're always fussing–doing things–you drove me nuts–sometimes at night, when I was sleeping, I could feel you looking at me–pulling the blankets up under my chin–even straightening my pillow –whether I wanted it straightened or not."

She bowed her head to hide the tears; it was true, she was a born fusser. When she loved someone she wanted to do everything for him.

He asked, "Could I have another roll? And some coffee? I don't suppose you have any of that carrot cake? Or molasses cookies?"

She jumped to her feet. "I'd like some coffee, too. I have some cinnamon rolls in the freezer. It'll just take a few minutes to thaw them over the wood stove."

"If you had a microwave like I suggested it would be a lot quicker," he said.

She didn't comment, but as she tended to the rolls, she thought, "If he wanted a microwave so bad, why didn't he buy one?"

When she brought him his rolls he was slouched in his chair as if he never intended to get up. He motioned to his tray. "Get rid of this, will you? Where's that little table we used to put stuff on?"

"I'll get it." She set up the table, then scurried back to the kitchen with his tray as the water for coffee came to a boil. The radio announcer warned of a major blizzard burying the city and surrounding areas. Several main roads were closed. Her heart fluttered as she realized that in all probability Wally would be trapped for many, many hours, maybe overnight. Could this be fate? He would realize how nice it was to be with her, how comfortable, he would realize how much he loved her. She would never, never mention his fling with Judy. All would be as it used to be. She closed her eyes, switching off the radio, leaning against the sink and wishing hard for everything to turn out the way she wanted.

"Hey! Where's the coffee?" Wally yelled.

As she poured his coffee she said, "Wally, I think you'd better wait until my plower comes before you try to get out."

He crossed his ankles and wiggled his toes, accepting the coffee with one hand and reaching for a warm bun with the other. "When do you think he'll get here?"

"I don't know." She did not want to tell him about the raging storm. His back was to the window. He looked so comfortable in his chair. Why spoil the moment? He would find out how bad it was soon enough. She thought of her cozy bedroom with the down comforter and the fireplace stacked with logs.

"I'd better call Judy," Wally said. "She's probably wondering where I am."

Judy will tell him about the storm, Beryl fretted, as Wally finished his coffee and went to the kitchen to make his call. He would see outside. Wouldn't he realize how bad the storm was? Or was he, his stomach full, his body warm, oblivious to the falling snow? She strained her ears toward the kitchen.

He said, "I have to wait for Beryl's plower, Judy. I could get my stuff in the car now so I'll be ready to go. What the hell do you mean, you don't want to hang around? Where could you go? Can't you just sit tight until I get back?"

He slammed down the receiver and came back into the living room, rumpling his hair. "Before I forget, did you find my navy blue suit? I need it."

"I took it to the cleaners."

"Why did you do such a dumb thing? Now I'll have to drive back out here to pick it up–unless–could you drop it off at my office?"

"Sure," she sighed.

"When do you think the plower will get here? I'll put these boxes in the car so I'll be ready to go," he said, getting into his coat and boots. "Come on and help me."

She stiffened. "No, I don't want to go out in that blizzard."

"Well–gee–there's four boxes here."

She piled the tray with the empty dishes and took it into the kitchen, the bubble of her dream bursting with the realization that what Wally wanted was to get back to Judy.

"No doubt you're the end of the line," he complained hours later. "You're probably his last job. Only you would live in this God-forsaken hole."

"You didn't complain last summer," she said, remembering how he had enjoyed swimming in the pond and sunning himself on the grass.

"That was last summer," he said crossly.

The phone rang. It was Judy asking crisply to speak to Wally. From his end of the conversation it was obvious that she was giving him a bad time. When he returned to the living room Beryl busied herself attending to the fire.

Finally he said, "Judy's sick and tired of waiting for me to get back. She thinks it's my fault I got stuck here. Like I want to! Give me a break! That dame has no understanding. She says she can walk to a nearby bar where some of the gang are waiting out this damn blizzard. She wants to have some fun. Boy, talk about being selfish."

She did not remind him that *she* would never go off to meet someone else, *she* would wait for him if it took forever. But then it dawned on her, Wally had never appreciated all she had done for him. As a matter of fact, he rejected her because of her all-consuming concern. It seemed to her that now he was complaining about Judy for the opposite reason, because Judy was so unconcerned. What, then, did he really want from a woman? Did he know?

Afternoon dragged into evening. Wally was hungry again. She made fried chicken, mashed potatoes, green beans and buttermilk biscuits, but her heart was not in it. She didn't care that there were little lumps in the gravy and ignored him when he complained. Something was wrong and she could not figure out what it was.

Wally pushed himself out of his chair only to call Judy. Finally, when he was getting no answer, he said he was giving up. "That's it. She's having herself a good old time somewhere." He flung himself on the couch, yawning.

Beryl washed the dishes and straightened up the kitchen. She glanced in to see that Wally had fallen asleep. Her immediate reaction was to cover him with an afghan–but–she didn't do it. Instead she polished the copper frying pan with salt and lemon juice and wondered why she had never asked him to help with the household chores, why he had just taken it for granted that she would wait on him hand and foot. Now, she thought, although he couldn't take *her* fussing over him, he was angry at Judy because *she* didn't concern herself at all with his needs. Funny, but even while these thoughts disturbed her, she hoped for some magic to work in the old farm house that night.

Eventually there was nothing else to do but to go to bed. He just shed his clothes and crawled in beside her and as eager as she was to be taken into his arms, she found a little seed of resentment taking root. Wouldn't you think he might think it was possible that she would not want him? Her thoughts were in a turmoil as they made love.

In the morning he fretted because all his clean clothes were in his car. He didn't want to get out of the warm bed and put his bare feet on the cold floor. He didn't want to have to go outside.

"Wrap yourself in a blanket," Beryl yawned, drowsy with love and, yet, astonishingly callous to his discomfort. She watched, amused, as he leaned out of bed, got his clothes from the floor and shivered into them under the covers.

"Aren't you going to start that fire?" he whined.

"The kitchen will be warm," she said. "It only takes a few minutes to get the one in the living room going. The whole house will be warm before you know it."

He spent all that morning trying to call Judy, finally giving up in a temper. Beryl did not comment. A state of emergency was announced over the radio. They agreed they were lucky to be safe in the house. For two days they read, played Scrabble and gin rummy and stared out the windows at the blowing snow. Beryl cooked and baked. They ate. She went out for wood. She cleaned up; he snored by the fireplace. They went to bed. Monday night she pushed him away. He pouted.

Tuesday morning she heard the snowplow coming up the driveway. Laughing, she leaped out of bed, stuffing herself into her clothes. She ran outside to ask the driver about road conditions, amazed at the relief that washed over her when she heard that traffic was getting through.

"If you have to get in the city you'd better get started before traffic gets heavy," the driver warned. "There might be a few more flurries this afternoon."

She rushed in to tell Wally. "Hurry if you want to get out of here."

Wally, burrowed up to his nose in the down comforter, did not answer.

Beryl attended to the fires and shook ashes down in the kitchen stove. She put the kettle on to boil and started a pan of oatmeal, singing gaily as she banged about.

Wally leaned against the door frame, unshaven and oddly quizzical as he looked at her. "Beryl–don't you think it was pretty nice–the two of us snowbound together?"

She covered the pan of oatmeal and put it on the back of the stove, hesitating, knowing that she could never tell him how her hopes had soared when she first realized they were going to be trapped together, knowing that she could never explain to him that if he had never left she would never have come to see that her life was better off without him.

"We couldn't stop the blizzard, could we?" she said. "You'd

better hurry, Wally. You don't want to risk getting stuck here again. You want to find Judy, don't you?"

"Oh–Judy–she'll show up sooner or later," Wally said. "You know, it's kind of funny, she doesn't even know how to fry an egg. And her refrigerator, it always has a sour smell. There's dust on everything, too. It's not nice like it is here."

"Well, everybody has their priorities," she said.

"Beryl–what if I did get snowed in again? I'm good company. Don't you think so? Don't you think I'm good company?"

She took a deep breath. "You're too much work, Wally. You don't pull your weight around here. You never did. Why would you want to get snowed in again? You hate it here."

"Beryl, maybe I just thought I hated it here. Maybe I wish I could come back," Wally said, his voice very low.

She handed him a mug of coffee. "Take this in the car with you. It'll help keep you warm until you can get some breakfast."

He opened his mouth to say something, but she hurried him into his coat and boots and shoved him out the door, smiling, pretending not to notice his reluctance. He spilled coffee on the snow as he went down the steps. Suddenly he lifted his arm, waved the mug wildly, then threw it at a tree. It spewed green glass and brown liquid through the serene white air. He brushed the snow off his car with long furious strokes, then climbed in and drove away.

Beryl did not watch Wally through the kitchen window. She ate her oatmeal sprinkled with brown sugar and made plans for the rest of the week. As soon as the roads were clear she would drive around the countryside, stopping at antique shops in her search for a blue willow bowl.

The Old Couple

The old man was stricken after the noonday meal. He pushed his chair back, got up from the table and lurched forward, a gurgling noise in his throat, catching his fall with big-knuckled hands spread flat on the table. Millie heard him from the kitchen sink as she squirted Ivory Liquid into the dish water, but she did not turn around until he gasped her name.

"Millie–"

"What do you want?" she demanded, studying his ashen face, recoiling from the noise of his raspy breathing.

"I'm having an attack," he mumbled, watery blue eyes scared under the heavy visor of his bushy gray brows.

"You're always having an attack," she said, but she noticed the beads of perspiration on his upper lip and wondered if this one could be for real, then turned back to the window over the sink and looked out at the snow blowing across the yard, piling up in drifts against the garage.

"Help me to my chair," Henry wheezed.

Millie, a tiny bird of a woman, barely came to his shoulder, but, grudgingly, she grasped his arm and shuffled with him to the front parlor where he dropped into his shabby brown chair.

He rumbled, eyes accusing, "Maybe it's that damn cabbage."

"It's what you wanted," she bristled.

"You probably didn't cook it long enough."

"I cooked it as long as I always do, and what would you know about how long cabbage should be cooked? When have you ever done anything in the kitchen but shovel it in?"

"I know enough to know it wasn't cooked until it was good and done, that's what's giving me gas around my heart, why didn't you just throw it on my plate raw? It would have been just about the same thing," he growled, wiping the sweat off his face with the back of his hand. "I can feel it all around my heart. Gas. That's what it is. Gas. You didn't cook the cabbage long enough. Always in a hurry so you can watch your damn program. What do you care if I get gas, you don't feel it knocking around in your chest. I noticed you didn't eat much, probably knew you didn't cook it long enough."

"I cooked the cabbage long enough, that's for sure, and as for being in a hurry, you're the one who wants his dinner twelve sharp every day," Millie snapped. "You're the one sniffing around the kitchen, wanting to know when dinner will be on the table, afraid you won't get it at the stroke of twelve."

He struggled for a breath. "I'm entitled to my hot dinner at noon after working my butt off all those years, eating cold sandwiches every day while you could do as you pleased."

"Sure, I did what I pleased every single day and the washing and ironing and cleaning and cooking got done all by itself," she sneered. "And all six kids got raised by themselves while I just flitted around having myself one grand old time."

"Shut it up, you always had a smart mouth," he said, his head lolling on the back of the chair, one hand massaging his chest. "It's gas, that's what it is, gas around my heart. I can feel it rolling around."

Without another word, she left him to finish her kitchen chores and make a cup of tea to enjoy with her program. Henry was snoring noisily so she turned the TV volume up. It would have been better if she had gotten him to bed. Then she wouldn't have to look at him or listen to him. As if, after almost sixty years of catering to his appetite, she did not know how long cabbage should be cooked. He always had been one to find fault, to complain, to think things could be better, but he had seldom been the one to try to better things. He had trudged through life as if he had been struck one hard blow after another.

She lost herself in the trials and tribulations of the inhabitants of Pine Valley while storm warnings flashed across the bottom of the screen. She paid no attention to the blizzard update. What did she care if it snowed all week? She wasn't going anywhere.

Henry snored on and Millie felt herself nodding off a couple of times, but she snapped out of it and forced herself to watch the end of "All My Children", even though, since Jenny died years before, she did not have the same enthusiasm for the soap opera. They could have had Jenny and Greg move out of Pine Valley, they didn't have to make Jenny die just because the actress who played the part wanted to leave the show. Well, Millie thought, as she snapped off the TV and glanced at her husband, she supposed the writers were sometimes stumped for new story lines.

She went to the telephone and called her only daughter who lived a few miles away. Darlene told her the city was still paralyzed by the blizzard. Hundreds of people were trapped in their homes or offices because of the snowstorm.

"Ma, don't you listen to the news?" Darlene asked.

"They always exaggerate," Millie said.

"Ma, this is no exaggeration, "Darlene insisted. "Do you need anything? Do you have enough food in the house?"

Millie grinned. What a dumb question. What if she didn't have enough food? Who would get it to her? She and Henry had been housebound since Saturday afternoon when the storm first hit. Usually one of their sons came with his snowblower to dig them out, but this time nobody had been able to come to their rescue. Besides, she hadn't really thought about it. She had no place to go. Neither did Henry. Snowed in or not, it made little difference to her.

Millie said, "We don't need anything. You know, I made cabbage for dinner and your father accused me of not cooking it long enough. As if, after all these years, I don't know how long to cook cabbage. Imagine. He said it gave him gas around his heart. Isn't that a laugh, him telling me how to cook? When did he ever so much as peel a potato, that's what I'd like to know."

"Gas around his heart," Darlene repeated. "Ma, where's Dad now? What's he doing?"

"He's snoring in his chair just like he always does after he stuffs himself with his dinner."

"Are you sure he's all right?"

"Didn't I just say he's snoring?" Millie was irritated. She didn't want to waste her daily call to her daughter discussing her cantankerous husband.

"Why don't you set my mind at ease and check on him before I hang up?" Darlene urged. "You know he's been acting kind of funny lately. You don't want to take a chance."

"All right," Millie agreed, placing the receiver on the table. She did not get up from her chair. Acting funny lately? Ha! Henry had acted funny most of his life if you asked her. She rapped her knuckles on the back of the chair and hoped it sounded like footsteps. She'd be darned if she'd get up to go and check on him when she could hear him snoring. She rustled the church bulletin faintly, grinning, thinking it might sound like rustling skirts on the other end of the phone. She picked up the receiver again.

"He's fine, sleeping like he always does after dinner. So, tell me, what have you been up to?" Millie firmly changed the subject.

They talked for a few minutes, then Millie went to the kitchen to gaze out the window at the blustery sky. She knew from long, long experiences with Buffalo winters that this would not go on forever. She did not mind being trapped in the house. There was plenty of food, her knitting and the TV. Although this was Tuesday, the fourth day of the storm, and she was hankering for someone besides Henry to talk to. Her son Kyle had called that morning and promised to get around with the snowblower as soon as possible. Millie reflected, having six kids in nine years might have been grim at the time, but it was having its payoffs in her old age. She felt sleepy, wondered if she should indulge herself with a nap, and decided she would watch the Home Shopping Channel. She liked to see what was up for sale and what people would be foolish enough to buy. She was nodding off when she was startled by Henry's guttural voice.

"Millie–it's so dark–so early–"

"It's not dark," she said, rousing crankily from her snooze. "It's still snowing. There are huge drifts across the front as well as the back. Why don't you get yourself up and take a look instead of drooping around all afternoon? See what's going on in the world?"

"Huh? What did you say? What–do you do–watch that damn boob tube–" Henry struggled to get up from his chair, his mouth hanging slack, a glob of spittle glistening in one corner.

Millie observed her husband disgustedly. How careless he was becoming. He didn't care that he was drooling and now let out an explosive belch. He had become so lazy he could hardly push his long, stooped body up from his soft chair. His left arm hung limply over the edge of his chair. She turned her attention to the TV, half-listening, half-dozing as she watched Hummel figurines being displayed for sale, until she heard strangled sounds coming from her husband.

"What? Henry?" Millie jumped.

"Can't–get–up," he stuttered, terrified.

Finally alert to his distress, Millie flew to him, the awful truth dawning on her as she saw him sprawled in his chair. He did not have gas around his heart from under-cooked cabbage, he was suffering either a stroke or a heart attack. "I'll call one of the boys–no–I'll call an ambulance–I'll call–"

"No!" Henry barked, his chest heaving. "No–hospital –no–ambulance–no–"

"There's something terribly wrong, you've got to see a doctor," Millie persisted, frightened, feeling an urgent need to get medical attention for him. Outside the parlor window the storm had lessened, but, although the plows had gotten through earlier that day, the streets were clogged with snow. The driveway was piled high across the middle. How could she manage to get him out of the house and to a hospital? She started for the telephone.

"Millie! Don't!"

It was a command, reminding her of days long past when he had been the young husband and she the young wife and he would get angry with her. "Millie! Don't!" he used to shout the same command and sometimes she stopped whatever it was he objected to and sometimes she didn't. This time she stopped. Instinct told her he was having some kind of an attack that could be fatal, but that he was no longer afraid and if this was the end for him he wanted to die in his own bed. Once, in one of the rare congenial moods of their old age, they had discussed dying, promising each other not to prolong one another's lives. No tubes and machines for them when their time came. They were both well past eighty and when the Good Lord called them they were willing to go. But not in a sterile hospital surrounded by doctors and nurses, needles poking in their arms, tubes shoved up their noses, machines pumping their breath in and out.

"Get– me– to– my– bed." His breath whistled faintly between rigid lips, his upper plate slipped down so that he looked like he was grinning.

They made the slow, stumbling way to their bedroom, Henry hanging on to her brittle body, clutching for balance at the walls and furniture, knocking over a lamp, swearing, grunting, sweating. They could not manage to get his clothes off, they were both so exhausted. He lay with his eyes closed, breathing laboriously. She pulled a chair to his side. It was the least she could do now. For all the anger and bitterness, for all the disappointments and broken dreams, for all the futility and drudgery of their life together, they were bound together as husband and wife. Once they had lain together on this very bed in feverish passion. No matter that it had been years since they had turned to one another in the night, the memory of their youthful love-making was suddenly and vividly there in the bedroom with them.

Millie wiped the corner of his mouth with her handkerchief. His eyes fluttered open, he tried to say something, but the power of speech was now beyond him. No matter, she caught the expression in his eyes and knew–oh, how she knew–that he was remembering the same days.

His harsh breathing filled the room as shadows lengthened into night. She held his cold hand between her bony ones. Death was no stranger to her. Millie was not afraid, and, as fatigue washed over her in gigantic waves, she was almost envious that Henry's spirit would soon soar free of his deteriorating body. She studied the frost patterns on the window, her mind playing tricks on her as she wandered in and out of dozing, seeing old, familiar faces in the icy formations. As the wind rattled the glass and sent tree limbs scratching the side of the house, she heard voices long since gone to their graves. Were they calling to Henry? Did he hear the voices, too?

Millie's mind groped in the past, picking up bits and pieces, dreaming of how she and Henry had been in the early days of their marriage. There were tender moments then that somehow got lost in the terrible depression. Ah, those were hard, hard times and they had never recovered from them. They had struggled to put food on the table for their growing brood and had considered themselves lucky that Henry had been able to find odd jobs when the auto plant closed down, lucky that she had been able to make money sewing. Those had been years of hardships and fears.

Was that what had crushed their dreams and their love, was that what had made them hopeless and angry, turned their love into loathing for one another? Because her beauty had faded, her bright, shiny brown hair had grown dull and limp, his shoulders sagged under his burdens, their teeth decayed because they used whatever money they could scrape together to buy shoes for the kids instead of going to the dentist.

Through her tears, Millie gazed sadly upon her husband, in a flash of clarity recognizing the truth. Those hardships would never have destroyed them if they hadn't forgotten how to love. They had allowed life to defeat them, turn them into a hostile old lady and a wretched old man because they had not remembered to fan the flame of their love.

Henry's breathing grew more shallow. Was he aware that she was there or was he beyond caring? Millie stood up, swaying with exhaustion, stiff joints creaking as she slipped off her shoes and crawled under the blankets beside him. They were too old and worn out for passion, but it was not too late to comfort one another and, in that moment, as she pressed her scrawny body against the bulk of his, courage surged through her with as much force as the desire that had once driven her into her young husband's arms.

A Cloud Slipped Across The Moon

"It's just not in them to stick around. They aren't made that way. After they've had their shoes parked under your bed for awhile men get the itch to park them some place else. That's just the way it is. Accept it."

Her mother was trying to cheer her up, but, swollen with misery, Ava could only zero in on the awful truth that Larry had left.

She lifted her head from her folded arms on the kitchen table, stared at the remains of their dinner and wondered why he had chosen to gobble up the lamb chops, buttered broccoli and fried potatoes before he belched and announced loudly:

"I'm going, Ava. We aren't getting along so why should I stick around?"

He was so matter-of-fact that at first she didn't realize the implication of his words. She scrambled to put things right. "You mean because of the rent money?"

Larry had not given her his share of the rent for almost a year. He hadn't contributed to the groceries either. She had been supporting them, resentfully at times, angrily most of the time, complaining all the time. Now her mind darted back and forth, trying to find excuses for both of them–him for free-loading, herself for nagging him to pull his weight. But his eyes, once so warm and loving, stared coldly into hers and her heart shivered and dropped into the pit of her knotted stomach.

"Where are you going?" she asked.

He stretched, yawned and pulled on his leather jacket. "I'm moving in with Ben until I can get a place of my own."

"Oh, live off him for awhile," she said.

"There you go again–gotta get in your digs, don't you?" he said, his upper lip curling.

She retorted, "What about all the money you owe me for your share here?"

"What about it?" Larry stared at her, blue eyes prominent.

"You gonna take me to court? Sue me?"

Ava laughed harshly. "Lot of good that would do me. You can't make someone give what he doesn't have."

"Oh, I got it all right," he grinned. "I just didn't give you any. Rather spend it on something worthwhile."

She grabbed a stalk of broccoli and threw it at him. "Get the hell out of here!"

He threw the broccoli back at her, smacking the side of her head, laughing as she grimaced. "Thanks for the lamb chops." The door slammed behind him.

Her eyes fogged with tears, she dialed her mother who would be better in this emergency than any of her friends. Hazel had gone through four husbands of her own, the second one Ava's father who was a dim figure, having packed up and scooted off when she was three years old.

"You'll get over him," Hazel said as she collected the dirty dishes and scraped dried up potatoes and congealed lamb fat into the garbage. "The first thing you ought to do is go out shopping for some snazzy clothes, then have your hair done. Next, go out and meet some new men. Take your time before you settle on one, the pickings aren't that great."

In spite of her heartache, Ava laughed. "Just like that?"

"Just like that," Hazel snapped her fingers. "Unless, of course, you want to sit around moping and driving your friends crazy talking about that bum. What's over is over, why waste time stewing over it?"

" I love him," Ava protested, but even as she said it she knew it wasn't true. Larry had been getting on her nerves for months and more than once she had been on the verge of throwing him out, but he always seemed to sense when he had gone too far and was clever at making her forgive his shortcomings, usually by making love to her. He was good at that, all right. Making love made her feel better about everything and she always temporarily forgot what is was about Larry that made her so damn mad.

"What you ought to do is pack up his things and put them outside the door. Call him and tell him to pick them up," Hazel said. "Don't open the door for him, don't let him get his foot inside."

Ava shook her head. "I'm not going to do all that work. Let him come and get his own things."

"Not a good idea, hon. If he comes in the apartment he will spy other things he'll want and you won't be able to stop him from grabbing things. Get his stuff outside, change the locks and don't let him in."

She admired her mother's approach to the situation. Experience obviously made Hazel practical in this kind of a situation. Ava did not remember her father leaving, and, of course, she had never known her mother's first husband, but numbers three and four had been a large part of her growing up. She had called the third one "dad" and the fourth one Pete. After Pete had departed for parts unknown (he was a bottom-of-the-barrel saxophone player) there had been a series of live-in boy friends. Hazel had sworn off marriage by that time.

"The only reason a woman should get married is to have a baby," she concluded. "A baby should be legitimate, but, after that, it doesn't make sense to tie the knot. It's too much trouble to get a divorce. To tell you the truth, hon, you're the only good thing that came out of any of my men. I'm glad I have you."

But Ava decided when she was in her teens that her mother had to be wrong about men. She knew there were couples who stayed married, her friends' mothers and fathers, for example. Besides, she read romance novels and they always ended with the hero and heroine in a passionate embrace. Ava knew she wanted one man in her life forever; it had to be better than the way her mother had lived. When she found the perfect man she would do everything to make him happy so he would never want to leave.

She was in such a hurry that she didn't see Larry's flaws at first. He was tall, broad-shouldered, had a head of blonde curls, poutty red lips and bold blue eyes. He loved to dance. That's how they met. Ava went with her girl friends to a popular bar with a band on Friday and Saturday nights. That Saturday evening singles on the prowl were three deep at the bar, sizing each other up. She saw Larry first. He was watching the door to see if anything better than what was already there would come prancing through. As he swung his eyes away from the door he caught Ava's glance. The band began playing. He beckoned to her, not even bothering to walk over and ask for the dance.

She ignored him, looking down into her glass of Chardonnay, her heart beating faster. He was gorgeous. She wanted to dance with him, but she would not allow herself to be summoned. She was conscious of his approach. He touched her arm and she tipped her glass to her lips.

"Hey! How about a dance?"

She put her glass down on the bar, knowing she would never resume drinking from it. All sorts of germs could be transmitted from a glass; you never knew who might sneak a sip from a temporarily abandoned glass of wine. She had always been careful about things like that. It was the way she had been brought up. Her mother might not be too particular about men, but she was always wary of germs.

Larry took her hand and led her to the dance floor. At first she had trouble following him, but he applied pressure to the small of her back with his hand and she soon read his signals. He was so tall. She felt the way all women feel in a tall man's arms, protected and feminine.

They danced all night, but when the bar was closing down she shook her head at his offer of a ride home. "I came with my girl friends and we always leave together."

"Take care of one another so you don't get into trouble, huh?" he asked. He had a wicked grin. He was a little drunk, but he was not nasty. "Do you girls have a rule about giving a guy you meet in a bar your telephone number?"

"We never give out telephone numbers the first time we meet a guy," Ava said primly, although this was not true. She decided it might be a good idea to keep Larry dangling for awhile, not be too easy. She had seen the other girls watching him all night, saw that he was popular and could dance with any girl he wanted.

"It was fun," he said, backing off with a grin. "I'll see you around?"

"Maybe," she said, and then added, so as not to seem unattainable. "You're a great dancer. I enjoyed the evening."

All the next week she planned for their next meeting. Of course the next time she let him drive her home, but she said goodnight at the door. She wanted to be very careful before she committed herself to Larry, no matter how strong the attraction. She had seen her mother gather up men as casually as she might have picked out a new dress, worn it and then discarded it without a second's thought. She vowed she wasn't going to do that. When she met the right man she was going to be certain it lasted.

That's why she hesitated about letting Larry move in with her. Ava believed in marriage, but Larry said the usual thing, that marriage was just a piece of paper. That statement had become a cliche among her friends, but she had to swallow it if she wanted to keep him. She convinced herself that after they lived together for awhile Larry would decide he wanted a legal commitment.

His contribution to Ava's apartment was himself. He had no stereo equipment, no TV, no radio, no furniture of any kind. He arrived with a bag of dirty laundry.

"You don't mind, do you, sweetheart?" He dumped the dirty laundry at her feet, kissed her ear and worked his way around to her lips. "You can throw it in with your own."

She squirmed when she remembered that she had been more than happy to do his laundry, to cook for him, to clean the apartment, to run his errands. Men, she had thought indulgently, were really helpless little boys. She planned to make herself so indispensable to him that he would never think of leaving her.

"Your husbands all walked out on you because you didn't take care of them," she told her mother.

"If you mean I didn't wait on them hand and foot, you're right," Hazel said, watching her daughter fold Larry's socks at the kitchen table. "You hold down a full time job, too, why should you come home to another? He should pull his weight around here."

Ava smoothed out a pair of sweat socks. "I think I should have soaked these in bleach. What do you think?"

"I think you should soak his head," Hazel replied, but there was no bitterness in her voice. She was simply stating how she felt.

Ava had convinced herself that where her mother had gone

wrong was in not catering to her man of the moment. A man liked to come home to a clean place with dinner on the table and his laundry folded and put away in his bureau. He liked a woman who cared for him so much that she made him apple pies and chocolate cakes. Ava was that kind of a woman.

Things started to go wrong when her budget strained supporting both of them. A woman liked to dress up for her man, too, but more and more she found she could not afford the pretty clothes she coveted. Larry paid his share of the rent for three months, then, apologetically, said he was a little short. He was a little short when it came to contributing to the groceries, too. He was good about bringing home a bottle of wine and he could always soften her up with Reese's peanut butter cups or, more romantically, a single red rose. When he was romantic she pushed bad thoughts out of her head.

"If we love each other, money should never be an issue," Larry said." True lovers pool everything, they don't say 'this is mine' and 'this is yours'."

In her heart she believed this to be true, but her head told her something was wrong with his reasoning because they were not pooling anything, they were just using what was hers. She began to snap at him, turn a cold shoulder in bed, neglect his laundry and demand that he at least take the garbage to the dumpster.

"I think you're just using me," she screamed at him one night.

He stalked out of the apartment and she was actually relieved. An hour later he reappeared with a bottle of wine and a bouquet of yellow tulips. He knelt at her side, put his head in her lap and begged her to love him. She put her hands in his blonde curls and sighed.

After great sex that night she was reluctant to ask him for his share of the rent. Somehow it seemed like asking to get paid for sex. It was indecent.

Hazel suggested she make a list of complaints and give it to Larry to read.

"If you want to keep the bum, soften it up with a letter. Give it to him to read, tell him you'll go for a walk and you'll be back in an hour. It'll give him time to think about what you have to say."

Ava thought that was a good idea. She wondered if her mother had ever done that with any of her husbands or boyfriends? Larry, when she gave him the letter, grunted and asked her to get him a cold beer.

She stiffened. "Larry, why can't you get your own beer?" Then, contrite, she hurried to the refrigerator. "I mean–sometimes I think you should wait on yourself."

He grabbed the beer and stared at the letter in his hands. "Why did you write me a letter? What's this all about?"

"Well, it's just some things I want to say to clear the air." Ava felt her stomach quiver. "I'm going to go for a little walk and when I come back we'll have a talk about–well, you know?"

"Huh?"

He looked so gorgeous, blonde hair curling around his ears, his lower lip in a pout, that she almost ran to him and hugged him instead of leaving him with the letter. When she came back from her walk the letter was on the floor and he was watching TV. "Well?" she asked, tense, but hopeful.

"What was that pile of shit all about?" he demanded.

She was determined to remain calm."Some things I think we should talk about."

"Talk all you want, I don't have to listen." Larry turned the volume of the TV up. "I like things the way they are and I've got nothing more to say."

Ava went to bed with a book and when he crawled in beside her she put the extra pillow between them. "Suit yourself," he growled and fell asleep. In the morning she told him to make his own damn breakfast and slammed the door behind her.

She didn't want Larry living with her any more, but she didn't think she could live without him. If only he would change, contribute his share of the finances, at least pick up after himself, maybe they could work things out. But he was obstinate and she was becoming just as obstinate. She left his dirty laundry in the hamper, refused to clean up after him and never made him breakfast. She stopped baking pies and cakes. They began eating out most nights or bringing home take-out.

"What's going on here?" Larry asked one night, eating fried rice from a paper carton. "I miss those good meals. What's bugging you?"

He looked so sad, like a little boy who didn't understand what was going on. She thought she might be carrying things too far, but then she thought maybe he had finally realized he had to shape up. How long could she hold out, not cleaning the apartment, not cooking, not doing his laundry? But she was also tired. She worked hard, the computers at the travel agency had been down for most of the day and the office had been hectic. She hardened her heart and said nothing. He dribbled sweet and sour pork down his chin and she turned away in disgust.

Why didn't she throw him out? She had tried appealing to his sense of fairness, but he had ignored her. She had left his messes in the apartment and he stepped over his dirty clothes or kicked them out of his way. Nothing seemed to be working. Maybe, she thought, if she cooked him a nice dinner, lamb chops and broccoli, he would soften up and they could have a real talk, get to the bottom of what was going on between them.

She had had one last desperate hope.

Now she watched her mother put away the clean dishes and mop up the sink with the dish cloth. "This place could use a good scrubbing," Hazel said.

Ava was thinking about Larry. She wished she could have scrubbed him up, rinsed away all his bad habits as easily as her mother had cleaned up the kitchen.

The telephone rang and they both jumped.

Ava picked up the receiver.

It was Larry.

"Ava," he said, "I've been thinking, if you start treating me better I might be willing to take another stab at it."

Her eyes met her mother's. "Did Ben throw you out?" she asked.

"No, Ben didn't throw me out. He said I could stay as long as I want," he said. "But, I miss you already. Walking out the way I did, that was a dumb thing for me to do. If you promise to quit nagging I'll come back. How about it?"

"No," she said. "It's over between us, Larry." She hung up

and smiled at her mother. "It *is* easy, isn't it?"

Hazel gave her a hug. "It gets easier every time, hon."

But why, then, after her mother had gone, did she feel so blue? She sat at the kitchen table with a glass of milk, not thinking about Larry, but about her own father and the other men who had walked out of her mother's life and so out of hers. It seemed to her at that moment that all her life she had longed for a family, a feeling of permanence. Romance and love had been part of it, but the real search had been for someone to fill that empty spot in her heart.

She went to the sink to rinse out her glass.

She opened the window for a breath of fresh air and looked up at the sky.

A cloud slipped across the moon.

Sunday Morning Sex

Everett's story:
When I told Sharon I wanted a divorce I could tell by the way she met my eyes that a divorce was just what she had been hankering for.

So I asked her why she hadn't said anything.

She looked down at her desk where she had been writing and for a few seconds I thought she was going to go back to work without answering me, just shrug her shoulders and act like the divorce was a done deed. She's always been like that, able to ignore whatever it is she doesn't feel like dealing with at the moment. Once I thought it was an endearing trait, it made her seem kind of vulnerable, but at that moment she just irritated me, but then for the last few months just about everything she did irritated me. Maybe I get under her skin, too. I know it drives her crazy when I park myself in front of the TV and guzzle beer and drop pretzel crumbs between the sofa cushions.

Her reaction when I told her I wanted a divorce was so typical. Was she devastated? No. She finally looked at me out of those pale greenish slanted eyes and the message I got was "Okay, I want a divorce, too." Of course she didn't say it, she tapped a pencil on the poems scattered across the desk, heaved a sigh and sat back to hear what else I had to say.

Well, how do you respond to someone like that? In the years we've been married I've never figured her out. I never figured out her poems either. She wins prizes for some of them, but I swear I don't know why, most of them make no sense to me. My feelings for Sharon make no sense to me either. Half the time she acts like I don't even exist. Maybe I thought if I asked for a divorce that would shake her up and make her pay more attention to me, but she just agreed to a divorce without actually saying so.

So what could I do after that except say that I'd pack a few things and leave?

"Where are you going?" she asked, taking off her glasses and rubbing the bridge of her pointed nose.

"I don't know," I sulked. "I haven't thought that far."

"What's the hurry? You might as well stay until you find a place," she said, and I swear there was absolutely no emotion in her voice; it was as if I had told her I was sore because there was no chocolate fudge ice cream in the freezer.

So that's how I ended up staying on, even though I asked for a divorce and even though I plainly saw that it made no difference to her. On the other hand, she told me there was no hurry and to stick around until I found a place to live. Of course she knew I'd never leave after that, so wasn't that a way of saying stick around forever? She didn't throw me out of our bedroom. And Sunday morning she didn't push me away when I showed her what I wanted before we had our bagels and cream cheese.

We met at a bowling alley. When she gets what she calls writer's block, she likes to bowl two or three games. She throws a lot of gutter balls. I've never known her to get a strike or a spare, although she says she has on occasions. Her top score was 92. That night she bowled on the alley next to where I was with three of my buddies. We were fascinated by the way she glided to the foul line and clunked the ball down the alley. She never stayed to watch, but returned to the rack to wait for her ball.

That's how I started a conversation with her. I asked, "Don't you like to see how many you knocked down?"

"Why should I? There's an electronic scorekeeper," she replied, but she smiled and I could tell she knew we had been watching her.

That broke the ice and after we had all bowled our last game I asked her to stay for a drink. There's no denying I was captivated by her, and Sharon seemed amused by me. She didn't talk much so I rambled on about my job as a sales rep for a manufacturing company and how I was on the road a lot and how my buddies and I frequently bowled late at night because that was a good time for us to get together.

When she told me she wrote poetry, of course I remembered how I hated reading poetry in school, but I didn't think then that she meant that's what she did full time. I thought she meant she wrote poetry the way some women make little ceramic dishes or knit sweaters, you know, a hobby. When I asked her out for Saturday she said she was doing a reading. I didn't know what that meant, but I didn't want to show my ignorance so I said okay, I'd try her again some other time.

The guys kidded me about my attraction to her. She's taller than me, skinny as a rail and has long floppy light brown hair, but she does not look like a geek and, anyway, I'm used to going out with tall girls. How many girls in heels are shorter than five feet five? I haunted the bowling alleys for a few weeks, kidding around with her until I got up the nerve to ask for a date again.

"Where do you want to go?" she asked.

I usually asked a girl to dinner or to a movie or a concert, but with Sharon, I wasn't sure she would accept so I hadn't thought beyond the asking. She picked that up right away and that's one of the best things about Sharon, she's always been in tune to what I'm thinking, which is probably why she wasn't surprised when I told her I wanted a divorce.

She suggested a foreign film and I have to admit I enjoyed it after I got used to the sub-titles. Then we went to a bar in her neighborhood for drinks and sandwiches. I did most of the talking. She was a good listener, not like a lot of women who think they have to keep interrupting with comments and questions just to prove they are interested. Maybe that's what hooked me. I don't know any man who doesn't love to spout off about himself. She didn't mention her poetry until I said I'd like to read it.

"I don't like to share my poems with someone who doesn't appreciate poetry," she said with that quirky little smile of hers.

I protested vehemently," I can't appreciate your poetry unless you let me read it."

"Okay," she said. I came to her place for dinner the next Saturday and she gave me a book of her poems to take home. I couldn't make sense out of most of them, but I knew I was proud of her for writing them. Sharon was different from the girls I usually dated and I was proud of the difference, bragging about her "artsy ways" to my buddies.

It wasn't until we were married that I felt obligated to go to some of her readings.

Sunday Morning Sex
Mary Ann Eichelberger

    I was surprised to discover how many men were poets. One, a truck driver with a beefy face, wrote some steamy stuff. I liked it when the readings were in the back rooms of bars because these usually included a guy or a gal strumming on a guitar in between the poems. There was also plenty of wine and beer.

    When Sharon reads she sits on a stool with her poems in her hands. She has this way of tilting her head to one side that makes her appear shy, but I know she isn't shy at all, she's sizing up the audience. One time she read one of the few poems that I understood. I have a copy of it in my wallet.

Old Men At The Mall
They do time on benches in shopping malls
empty hands hanging between arthritic knees
or clasped on plaid flannel paunches, dim
memories mocking, faded eyes lusting
after young mothers in tight blue jeans
pushing babies in strollers, dragging toddlers
by one hand into bright caverns where
white haired women in polyester
pants suits paw through sales bins
until its time to search the benches at the
gurgling fountains and jewelry islands for
husbands in baseball caps who heave
themselves to their feet and shuffle off
to join hordes of

old men and old women and bored
young mothers with cranky children dragging
French fries through ketchup puddles, chewing
greasy hamburgers, sipping sugary drinks through

bent straws. Watching the passing
parade on the edge of their vision,
knowing they are destined to do more time
on their benches, old men reach
into yesterday for memories to dull the
ache that is the disappearing shadow of
themselves.

    I like that poem because it's such an accurate picture of what goes on in shopping malls, the old guys sitting there waiting for their wives to finish poking around in the stores, the little kids being dragged around by their mothers. At least that's the way I see things when I go to the mall early in the day, so I think Sharon said it all in that poem. What she says in the others is a mystery to me.

    I asked her to marry me after three months of dating. She said no, she didn't think so. "We're really very different," she said. "Besides, I couldn't handle marriage, all that togetherness. I like a lot of time to myself."

    "That's what would be so great about marrying me. I'm out of town a couple days a week, you'd have plenty of time for yourself," I said. I told her I was glad she liked time to herself, most women wouldn't like a husband on the road.

    I pushed my other argument home. "We could have a little house. It would be nice."

    "You can buy a house if you want to, but I don't care about owning property," she said. That's how she accepted my proposal.

    We got married in her folks' back yard. They call it a garden, but take my word for it, it's a back yard overrun with weeds. Her folks are nice people, but they don't care much for convention. Her father is always inventing something that doesn't work and her mother has been taking singing lessons for forty years and she's still waiting to be discovered. She sang "Because" at our wedding without paying the slightest attention to how it was being played on the keyboard, racing ahead or lagging behind the music.

    Her mother made Sharon's wedding dress out of some filmy

material that floated all around her. All I could think of was clouds and how beautiful my bride looked. When I told Sharon how I had felt she said it was very poetic.

I guess I loved her from the first moment I saw her in the bowling alley and I still love her. I think she loves me, too, but with Sharon it's kind of a funny thing, she doesn't need me and that makes me feel unnecessary. Or maybe I think that's a slap at my manhood. I don't think love is something you can explain, you either love someone or you don't, but I do think it helps to show it once in awhile, not take it for granted.

It gets me when I come home after being on the road for three or four days and she barely waves hello. I know she gets into that poetry and maybe it is hard to break off in the middle of an inspiration, but a man likes to think his wife is glad to see him. I will admit when she does have time for me she lets me go on for hours and shows an interest in my job. But the truth is she doesn't really care if I'm around or not. I don't know why we got married, unless you go back to where I said I love her. I don't have the answer, but I think our marriage is better than most of them I see. We never fight.

I think I knew when I asked her for a divorce that she would respond by wanting one too, but I didn't have any place to go so I stayed on. We never said another word about it. Sharon writes her poetry and drifts in and out of the house, I go to work and pack and unpack and leave her telephone numbers where she can reach me. She has never called me when I've been out of town.

Sharon still goes bowling late at night and if I'm in town I go along.

Sharon's story:
I didn't want to get involved with Everett. Men have a way of complicating things with their infantile demands to be fed on schedule and to have sex on Sunday mornings. What is it with men that they think sex is always better on a Sunday morning? You can never convince me that they think it is a religious experience.

My mother made my wedding dress; the material floated around my body inspiring me to write a poem about clouds because Everett said that's what he was reminded of when he saw me. I thought what he said was very poetic. It was the first and last poetic thing he ever said.

When my mother sang "Because" you could hear faint sniffling as my friends dabbed at their tears. I don't know if Everett's folks appreciated the beauty of the moment, but my family certainly did and my friends were misty-eyed long after the ceremony. The garden was a panorama of colors, flowers blooming everywhere. My father sows seeds at random so where most people have grass there were tall daisies and poppies and sweet peas. True, there were some weeds and scrubby patches where no seed had been sown, but that just added to the charm.

Everett's parents were very somber, but that didn't bother me. They live in a trailer park in Florida. I never have to see them again if I don't want to. I told my husband from the start that I wasn't going to get involved in Thanksgiving and Christmas dinners. My family has always been spontaneous and more often than not we celebrate the holidays when the mood is upon us, not on the official dates. We like to have Thanksgiving in the spring, as a way of saying thanks that we got through another winter. After all, what difference does it make what we are thankful for, so long as we remember to give thanks?

When my grandfather died he left my father more than a million dollars. My father quit his job and divvied the money up three ways, one third for him, one third for my mother and one third for me. It's all invested with the same broker my grandfather used and we all collect enough money to live comfortably.

I am a poet, but poets rarely make enough money to support themselves. Everett was surprised to learn this because I have six of my collections published. I explained to him that if it weren't for my inheritance I'd have to take a job to support myself. Money was never an issue between us. I put up half the money for the house he wanted and he put up the other half. He pays all the bills one month and I pay them the next. That was my idea. I don't need a husband to support me.

When we were first married he bought me expensive jewelry until I told him I didn't want it.

"I thought all women liked diamonds and gold!" he said.

"Not me, I don't want diamonds and gold," I said. "Besides, if I did want it I could buy it myself. I don't want you to give me things. Use your money to buy yourself a snazzy sports car."

He was a little hurt. I think he was trying to show me how much he loved me because he felt guilty about not attending my poetry readings after the first year. I assured him it made no difference to me whether he came to my readings or not, that I didn't expect him to change for me any more than I intended to change for him. We fell in love with one another just the way we are and I think we should be happy about our differences.

Everett is on the road several days a week and sometimes he is gone for one- or two-week stretches. I never miss him because I know he will come home and when he does I am glad to see him, but I don't get all sentimental about it. That's not my style, but sometimes, after he's been away, I initiate Sunday morning sex because it makes him happy and if he's happy, I'm happy.

It's really that simple.

As couples go we look odd together, I'm so tall and skinny and Everett is so short and scrawny. He insists he's five feet five, but like all short men he's stretching it a little. I don't really care, except when we dance. It's not very romantic to have his chin resting on my bony shoulder. The rest of the time, especially in bed, what difference does it make?

I've always felt relieved that Everett didn't get involved in my poetry. In the beginning he went to some of my readings and book signings, but he was usually so bored that it put me on edge. Without talking it over we decided it was best if we both went our separate ways in some areas. For example, I never cared what he was doing when he was out of town. It never once crossed my mind that he would be unfaithful and as for his job, I don't mind listening to him describe his involvement, I just don't want to have to comment.

We are an oddly matched pair with very little in common, but most of the time our marriage works. Things go awry when Everett compares us to other couples who do everything together. He has a sense of what he thinks is proper and that often causes friction between us. He accuses me of not knowing what a normal family is, implying that I was raised by a pair of crazies. I tune him out when he goes off on one of his harangues. Although more than once I retaliated by sniping that his parents are cold and stiff.

We irritate one another, but I think most couples do. It simply isn't possible to live in complete harmony with another person. There are a lot of things unsaid between us, areas we are both fearful of exploring. Never once did we discuss whether or not we wanted children. We were both in our mid-thirties when we married and I simply assumed he felt, as I most emphatically did, that we were too old to adjust to a child.

Divorce was another issue we never talked about. For a long time I had felt tense and unhappy when Everett was home. I wanted to scream at him when he plopped himself in front of the TV and guzzled beer hour after hour while I was trying to read or write poetry. He was like a child misbehaving just to get attention. Then, when I couldn't stand it anymore, I'd grab my bowling ball, thinking I could escape him for an hour or two, but he would snap to and insist on coming along. Sometimes when I flung the ball down the alley I pretended I was aiming it at his head.

It was no surprise when he said he wanted a divorce. I had been thinking that was the only option we had. But he had no place to go and, really, when I thought seriously about splitting up it didn't make too much sense. I made him his favorite dinner one night, stuffed pork chops and mashed potatoes and apple pie for dessert and then, when we were both feeling congenial, I asked him why we couldn't love one another just the way we were?

"I think that's what we've been doing," he said, squeezing my hand.

We just went on from there.

I never write love poems, I write poems about life. Life is love.

I wrote a poem as my gift to Everett for our fifteenth wedding anniversary.

Anniversary

Now in the autumn of our union
our fervent wedding vows
a dim memory
the desire that hurried
us to the altar waning
I search your familiar face
beneath your graying hair
and tracing each line
with affection gaze
into your eyes at
myself.

Everett gave me a new bowling ball for our anniversary. It's amazing how much better I bowl with a ball that's properly fitted. He carries my poem in his wallet.

Power Play

"Sooner or later I suppose every couple ends up where we are."

His face a mask of frozen hostility, Philip grunted in response to his wife's statement.

Elinore tipped her martini to her pink lips, her eyes studying him over the rim of the frosted glass. Predictably, he was reacting by imprisoning his thoughts in his brain, perhaps where they got tangled in that confusion of data which she sometimes imagined jammed his head. She observed the fingers of his left hand grasp a carrot stick. As he munched, she knew he craved cheese or salted nuts and resented her, not his doctor, for putting high cholesterol and high sodium foods on his forbidden list.

Elinore persisted. "It's true, you know. I think it's because there are no more ladders to climb. The thrill of the pursuit is over for you. It makes you rather anxious. That rubs off on me. After all, we made so many sacrifices for your career and I don't know about you, but I often wonder if it was worth it."

"Like you've had it so bad!"

She let his words dangle between them, between their icy martinis and the raw vegetables he loathed. She barely shrugged her shoulders, but he caught her gesture and was so infuriated that he snarled, "I'd like to know what you have to complain about!"

She took the fire out of him with one gentle word: "Nothing."

His eyes popped. He had steeled himself for an argument, but his wife failed to take the bait. He shifted uneasily in his leather chair, taking a long drink.

She explained, "I was merely trying to tell you how I feel. Now. At this particular stage of our lives. It occurred to me the other day when I was in the supermarket that not only have my shopping habits changed drastically in the last year or so, but so have both our lives. With the children grown and on their own, all the pressures of raising them are gone, and with you on the verge of retirement your career is no longer a priority."

Philip winced. She had struck a raw nerve. "I'm hardly on the verge of retirement. I have a few years before that."

"Not really. You must name your successor next year. Isn't that in your contract?" she asked.

It was times like this when he regretted sharing business details with her. She had a way of retaining every detail, which was frequently annoying. Early in their marriage he had been grateful for her avid interest, her suggestions, her encouragement and support. Although he had never acknowledged her contributions, he might not have made it to the top without her help.

"Isn't that true?" She drained her martini.

He stalled, refilling both their glasses. There was always the possibility that another drink would make her less irritating. He couldn't help a little smile, remembering how sexy she used to get when they were first married and she had had one too many cocktails. He paused in the act of straining ice from her drink, dim memories stirring vague, pleasurable sensations.

Elinore accepted her second cocktail, noting that her husband had not failed to add three anchovy-stuffed olives. He resumed his seat across from her, his martini floating a thin slice of lemon peel. Their eyes met, his wary. She sighed, wondering why their hour before dinner had turned into a battleground. Philip did not come home for dinner every night because he had so many business meetings, so on the nights he did come home he yearned for peace and yet, in spite of the fact that she knew this, she chose to draw the battle lines.

It was because they had grown so far apart. That was what she meant when she told him that she believed sooner or later every couple ended up where they were—a man and a woman co-existing not very harmoniously in a hollow atmosphere. Elinore knew that Philip was satisfied with the way things were simply because he did not want to do anything about their relationship. She had access to all their money, she enjoyed the status of the wife of a prominent executive, she was free to play golf all summer, vacation in Florida in the winter, visit their children whenever she pleased. He gave her everything but what she desired most: companionship.

She said, "I'm trying to tell you that I think we should spend more time together."

He scowled. "Where is this conversation headed, Elinore? It seems to me you're jumping all over the place. From harping about your dissatisfaction, to my retirement–to what? A plan for spending more time together? What the hell are you getting at?"

Facts were what he wanted. Hard, cold facts. He did not want to talk about how she felt, how he felt, how they had felt when they were first married, how they would feel next week, next month, next year. Elinore was grateful for her martini, if only because alcohol was better than Valium. It was futile to attempt to reach him, to tell him that she wanted to talk about the rest of their lives together. It was futile to try to explain to him that she felt lonely only when she was with him. In the early years she had not noticed that he was seldom there for her. In the beginning there had been the thrill of being newlyweds, the challenges of his job, the obligations to that job, then to their three children. The children had always been hers to care for. Philip did try to show up on parents' night at school, but frequently he was out of town. She had no time to be lonely then, or to notice that he was absent more than he was present.

She said, "I'm trying to tell you, Philip, that like so many couples our age we've become strangers to each other." She plunged ahead the way she would dive into the pool in their back yard, without hesitating in order to get the first shock of the cold water over with as soon as possible. After that, she could enjoy the swim.

The frozen mask clamped over his face again. He supposed there was nothing he could do but listen to her, hoping that she might get it out of her system. He wished he could explain to her that all day long he dealt with high-powered executives who were out for his jugular if he made one false move. When he came home all he wanted was to relax, eat dinner, read the paper, do some work at his desk and go to bed. He was not interested in discussions about their future, too exhausted to have her remind him that he was almost sixty, the obligatory retirement age in his contract. Why couldn't she use up her energies in aerobic classes, tennis–or in long discussions with her women friends? Why the hell couldn't she tire herself out so that on nights when he came home she would be just as eager for peace and quiet as he was?

He sat up straighter as she said, "I know you're tired, darling, I know you hate talking about us. I have a plan."

She watched him perk up. A plan? He thrived on plans. His entire life had been according to one master plan. She laughed softly at his sudden spark of interest.

"If you could just go over your schedule and see if you could find a few days when we could go away by ourselves—where there won't be any distractions. Maybe if it was just the two of us we could get in touch with one another again," she said.

Philip coughed. The last time she had made such a suggestion it had been in the hope they could rekindle their sex life. It hadn't worked. Their sex life was still non-existent. He simply couldn't perform. It happened to a lot of men his age. He deeply resented any desire on her part for sex. Damnit, if he couldn't give it to her, she should learn to live without it! But this time he was certain that she wasn't concerned with sexual fulfillment.

She forged ahead. "I feel as if we've lost touch with one another, like we simply co-exist in this house. I know we go out on weekends, but it's usually connected with business and even though we have a reasonably good time, it's not the same as the two of us planning to spend time together. Alone."

"What do you want to do?" he asked. His fingers tightened around the stem of his glass.

"Have a little vacation. Four or five days–over a weekend." She smiled. "Time for us to have nobody else to think about. Where we can get in touch with one another again."

This was the kind of proposition that made him squirm, made him stiffen with opposition while he calculated all the reasons why he could not oblige his wife. Board meetings. Deals he was working on. Meetings with the office staff. Year-end wrap-ups. Budget planning. Anything to veto her request.

Elinore's expression softened as she thought of long gone days when her parents moved in to look after their children while they went to business conventions, the only vacations they ever took. Mixing business with pleasure had not been difficult. The evenings after the banquets and the speeches always belonged to them to make love, to snuggle in one another's arms until dawn. How willing she had been then to be sweet to Philip's business associates, to make points with important executives, to lunch with their wives, knowing he was going to be all hers when they shut the hotel room door behind them.

He hedged. "I'm very busy at this time of the year. You know that." But in the circle of light from the lamp where she sat, his wife appeared unexpectedly vulnerable to him. His heart yearned toward her as it had not in a long, long time. He remembered how he had once done everything in his power to make her love him. Some long forgotten emotions stirred, making him defenseless against her request even as he balked at the prospect of fulfilling it.

She said, "You're busy all the time, but if you really want to you can find the time to go away with me for a few days."

He was weakening. "Where do you want to go?"

She smiled as she got to her feet. "Do you remember that little inn on Iroquois Lake where the Danvilles had their daughter's wedding reception last year?'

He did remember, and he recalled that she had said then what a delightful spot it was for a quiet vacation. That wouldn't be too bad. He mentally calculated that it would be a two-hour drive. He could manage to take a Friday off. They could leave after lunch on a Thursday and return the following Sunday afternoon. Yes, he could accommodate her, take her on a little vacation. That might keep her content for a long time – may be right through winter. It was October. He could arrange his schedule to take a long weekend. When they came back from their little jaunt Elinore would be busy making plans for Thanksgiving and then Christmas. There would be months of peace with a contented wife.

"Is that where you want to go?" he asked.

"Yes."

"I'll look into it," he promised, frowning. "Do you have your heart set on that particular place? If I can't get reservations do you mind if we go somewhere else?" If they went to New York he could squeeze in a few business meetings while she went shopping, write part of their vacation off as a business expense.

She was aware that the wheels of his mind were now in motion, that he was accustomed to making all the decisions and that he was already thinking of places he preferred to the little inn. It was a power thing with him. A show of authority. He was used to being in charge and he wanted her to acknowledge that this was his decision.

He was waiting for her answer, although for him her acquiescence was a mere formality. He was shocked to hear her reply firmly, "That's the only place I want to go. I'll call tomorrow and see about reservations."

She marched into the kitchen, put their dinner in the microwave, punched the buttons and took the salad from the refrigerator. She was dribbling dressing over the greens when he entered the kitchen to observe the final preparations.

When they sat across from one another at the polished mahogany dining room table with pale yellow plates on dark green mats, he looked with revulsion at the filet of sole sprinkled with paprika, the green beans and the medium baked potato without butter or sour cream. It was a low sodium, low cholesterol dinner, prepared to combat all the lunches and dinners he ate out, which presumably raised his blood pressure and clogged his arteries.

It appeared to Philip as he glared at Elinore that she was smirking, taunting him with her power. Here, in their dining room, she was the Chairman of the Board. He ground pepper over his food, secure in the knowledge that he would get his revenge. She could make all the plans she wanted for their little vacation, but he would triumph in the end.

He would not have a good time.

POEMS

BY

MARY ANN EICHELBERGER

Father

In his blue cardigan at 3 P.M.,
his gray head nods to his private lullaby
as my father gathers energy in his
ancient rocking chair, resting his eyes,
he says, so, when the evening paper comes,
he can digest the local news,
absorb world events, glance
at the obituaries for familiar names,
reassured by the sounds of my mother
cooking supper while he scowls at the financial page.

Often, in the twilight, he remembers the voices
of children, a time when four young faces
wreathed the dining room table. He wishes
there had been more time
to laugh, to play, to be together.
I tell him now that he gave
all that was in him to give
and it was enough.

MOTHER'S DAY

I will not come to your grave
bearing a bitter scented geranium
in a florist's clay pot,
or shed tears to nourish the grass
that would send its roots
in search of your soul.
I will not stand at your grave
filled with remorse, because
there was a time
I brought you tulips
the color of the sun
and purple violets and
bright pink azaleas from
the garden of my heart.

For My Son's Sixteenth Birthday

You cried
when I left you
hanging on as if to a life line
strong baby hands and chubby arms
wrapped like steel bands
around my legs. Then one day with a
wavering smile over your shoulder
you marched straight into that noisy room
with the slide and the building blocks.
Next year clutching a Spiderman lunch box
you trudged alone through the backfields
arriving at first grade triumphant!

Now on the eve of asking for my car keys
you don't cry anymore as you
plunge into the world
and I think it was good
that I pried your tiny fingers loose
kissed you goodbye and promised to return.
Will you?

First Grandchild

I did not know it would be this way,
that from the heart of my womb, where
once she floated serenely, blowing bubbles,
tugging at the umbilical cord, nursing on her thumb,
listening to my voice, her father's voice, the sound
of violins tuning up, the rustling of programs
before a concert...

I did not know it would be this way,
that from the heart of my womb I would
feel this quickening, this sensation I
cannot articulate as I embrace
my child, my daughter, hearing again the silenced
voice of my own mother and her father's
mother, and their mothers before them,
all the women who form the lifeline
to this newly conceived infant...

I did not know it would be this way,
that from the heart of my womb
would sing the voices of many women
rejoicing in my first grandchild.

WHEN YOU THINK I'M OLD

Someday, when you think I'm old,
please,
don't remember me at Christmas
with teeny jars of jam and honey,
waxy balls of orange cheese,
fuzzy slippers for what you assume
to be my cold feet.

Drink a martini
with me,
three olives in mine. I will
mix them. If I can no
longer do that,
bury me.

Someday, when you think I'm old,
please,
don't send me glittery cards,
lilies entwined with
rosary beads in praying hands.

Bring me a five-year calendar for
my ninetieth birthday. I'll hang
it by my desk, where
I'll be writing poems.

July Literary Press publishes fiction and poetry and theme-oriented collections. We are looking for stories and poems by and for the mature reader. We are not interested in pornography, nor any material that is, profane, sexist, racist or violent.

We are:

> Gay Baines, a free-lance writer, having abandoned her profession after thirty years. Her poems, short stories and essays have appeared in The Buffalo News, The Roycroft Review, Kiosk, Croton Review, Lullwater Review, and other publications. She has received several poetry awards, including first prize in the 1991 National Writers Union poetry competition and Honorable Mention in the Ruth Cable Memorial Poetry Award (ELF) in 1996. Her husband, political activist and writer W.H. (Ted) Baines, died in 1994. She is a member of the Roycroft Wordsmiths.
>
> Mary Ann Eichelberger, author of Is Mid-Life Easier In A Mink Coat? (Prometheus, 1989) a book of non-fiction based on her own life and interviews with women of the upper-middle income bracket. She has been published in Seventeen, The Buffalo News, The Writer, Elf, Z Miscellaneous, Poetry On The Buses, Poetry In The Libraries and various other publications. She is the mother of Clare Poth, an artist and teacher who did the cover painting for Storms. Clare is married to Tom Maynor who designed the website for July Literary Press. Mary Ann's son, Paul Poth, is Assistant District Attorney of Boston, MA.